T0014220

CLIMATE: OUR CHANGING WORLD

SCIENCE IN ACTION

CLIMATE: OUR CHANGING WORLD

ANDY SIMA
ILLUSTRATED BY **JENNY MIRIAM**

Albert Whitman & Company
Chicago, Illinois

To Randy, who kicked off the strange chain of events
that lead me here—AS

For Dexter, Céleste, and Iggy—JM

Library of Congress Cataloging-in-Publication data
is on file with the publisher.
Text copyright © 2023 by Andy Sima
Illustrations copyright © 2023 by Albert Whitman & Company
Illustrations by Jenny Miriam
First published in the United States of America in 2023
by Albert Whitman & Company
ISBN 978-0-8075-1206-7 (hardcover)
ISBN 978-0-8075-1203-6 (paperback)
ISBN 978-0-8075-1207-4 (ebook)

Photo credits: Public Domain, 16; Public Domain, 28; Public
Domain, 31; Public Domain, 31; Public Domain, 40; Photograph of
a water wheel, FOTO: FORTEPAN / Veszprém Megyei Levéltár/
Klauszer; People of Vanuatu, Graham Crumb/Imagicity.com, 67;
Public Domain, 77; Public Domain, 106; Public Domain, 107; Public
Domain, 112; "Wangari Maathai" by Oregon State University is
licensed under CC BY-SA 2.0. To view a copy of this license, visit
https://creativecommons.org/licenses/by-sa/2.0/?ref=openverse,
114; Public Domain, 133 ; Public Domain, 148–149; Public Domain,
162; Public Domain, 163; Public Domain, 170

Printed in China
10 9 8 7 6 5 4 3 2 1 WKT 26 25 24 23 22
Design by Kay Petronio and Erin McMahon
For more information about Albert Whitman & Company,
visit our website at www.albertwhitman.com.

CONTENTS

INTRODUCTION

··

Imagine you are a gardener working in a greenhouse with rows of plants in different shapes, sizes, and colors. Huge, spinning fans hum at either end of the greenhouse, making a cool breeze on your face.

Some plants are big, with tall stems and dark-green leaves. Some are thin grasses with delicate stalks and seeds at the top that wave back and forth. Other plants are short and squat, with sharp spikes. Insects crawl over them all.

You walk around, watering. Some plants need more water, some need less, and some barely need any.

Suddenly, you stumble, and your watering can gets caught in a fan. With a crash, the fan stops spinning. The end of your watering can is ripped to pieces. Using it, you pour too much water on the big plants, washing away some soil. You don't want to wash away the soil from the grasses, so you barely water them. You don't even try to water the plants with spikes; too much water would be catastrophic for them.

With only one fan, there is less cool breeze. The greenhouse is getting hotter. If you don't do something soon, your plants will die.

This may not be a familiar scene but, in some ways, a similar scene is playing out across our planet right now. The specifics are different but the idea is the same. Because of human actions, the world is getting hotter, and the weather

is less reliable. This is part of climate change, and it is having major effects on people and our world.

After years of research, scientists know that humans are causing Earth's temperature to rise. The world is getting hotter and drier in many places, making it more difficult to grow food. The world is getting wetter in other places, making people's homes less secure. Devastating natural disasters like hurricanes, tornadoes, wildfires, floods, and droughts are stronger and more common. Sea levels are rising, covering small islands. Coral reefs are dying. Forests are shrinking. Cities are polluted with smog.

Our world has many different environments, from rain forests full of birds to the driest deserts and, as the climate changes, each environment is affected differently. Climate change, also called global warming, makes life dangerous for people all over the world.

The word "environment" also refers to the whole earth. We need to look at many things to understand climate change: how it has happened, how it has damaged the environment, and what we can do to help. The earth is changing quickly because of climate change and we do not know what it will look like in five or ten years, but we know it will probably be different from today and likely more dangerous.

It may feel like the problem is so big that there is nothing we can do about it. But the good news about climate change is that because the problem is caused by people, we can fix it.

Everyone can help fight climate change, in different ways. And even though there are no easy solutions to climate change, we all need to help.

CHAPTER 1

WHAT IS CLIMATE CHANGE?

We see and hear that there are more storms, floods, and fires and higher temperatures in our world than ever before. These are all examples of the effects of climate change. Modern climate change is caused by too much carbon dioxide being added too fast to Earth's atmosphere—the air that surrounds our Earth.

Animals, including humans, release the gas carbon

dioxide into the air when we breathe out, and it is also released when animal and plant matter decay. It is also released when we burn fossil fuels, the fuels that are formed naturally in the earth, such as coal, petroleum, or oil, and natural gas. People burn too much fossil fuels so carbon dioxide is building up in our atmosphere. The carbon dioxide gets trapped in the atmosphere and causes the temperature to rise. This overheating of the atmosphere and our Earth causes climate change.

When we add too much carbon dioxide to the atmosphere, we cause climate change. We also cause air pollution that leads to health problems. Other gases also cause air pollution.

Air pollution contributes to climate change and it is also made worse by climate change.

Air pollution is only one cause of climate change but it is one of the most common issues that affects people.

Air pollution and climate change are separate problems with the same source.

Deforestation and ocean pollution are different from air

pollution and, like air pollution, they are major sources of climate change. At the same time, they too are also being made worse by the burning of fossil fuels that cause climate change. Deforestation and ocean pollution are global problems that contribute to the warming of the whole planet. Air pollution is more localized, occurring where fossil fuels are burned or certain kinds of chemicals are used.

CHAPTER 2

CLiMaTE, WEAThER, AnD ThE GREEnhOUSE EFFECT

Any problem related to climate change almost always has many other related problems.

Much of what we know about climate change comes from scientists who spend years studying the earth, learning as much about it as they can, and doing experiments to make sure their tests are accurate.

Possible solutions to climate change can create many new,

smaller problems, like how to move many people from one place to another or how to build stronger infrastructure or how to create new jobs for people, replacing ones that help create climate change. But even though the solutions may not be easy, sometimes they are necessary.

Climate change affects everything in our lives.

Climate and Weather

Earth's weather will, over time, become warmer and less easy to predict. This is already starting to happen, all over the world. To help understand how people are causing climate change and why the climate is changing, we need to understand the difference between climate and weather.

Two people are lying on a grassy hilltop, looking at cloud shapes. The wind blows slowly, moving warm summer air. The wind starts to blow stronger. More clouds appear, turning the sky gray. The wind gets colder, and so does the air. It starts to rain. The wind shakes the trees, and water covers the grass.

This sudden change from sunny skies to rain is an example of weather. Weather is what happens every day, and it includes things like the temperature and precipitation, such as rain, snow, or hail.

The difference between climate and weather is how long something takes. Climate happens over a long time across large distances. Weather happens over a short time in smaller areas. Weather measured over many years is called climate. If it is raining in both Chicago and Los Angeles, this is weather. But if your neighbor complains about it usually being cold and rainy in Chicago and wishes to move to the usually warm and sunny Los Angeles, this is climate. The weather may be the same in both cities that day, but the climates are very different. Scientists look at the average weather for a state or a country for a period of time to describe its climate.

If we look at all the weather on Earth, we can observe the planet's climate. Climate change means that Earth's average weather is changing.

The average temperature on Earth has increased about 1.9 degrees Fahrenheit since 1880, around the time when scientists were first able to get an average temperature for the globe. The average temperature now is about 57 degrees Fahrenheit. Most of this increase has happened since 1975.

This matters because when the earth is warmer, it speeds up the water cycle—the exchange of water among the oceans, the atmosphere, and land. Higher temperatures cause the water to evaporate faster, so soil dries out faster. And more water in the atmosphere means there is more rain or snow.

The first signs of changes in the water cycle are now showing. Since the beginning of the century, precipitation has increased by about 6 percent, and heavy downpours of more than two inches per day have increased by 20 percent. This can cause flooding, soil erosion, and loss of life in some areas of the world that are most affected. The increase in evaporation has led to drought in some places while heavy rain falls in other places.

Ecosystems are now reacting to warming. There are longer growing seasons for plants because the earth is warmer for longer periods.

Water expands when it is heated, so the rising temperatures

mean that sea levels have risen between 4 to 10 inches over the last 100 years. Glaciers are also melting, adding to rising sea levels.

Energy and the Greenhouse Effect

Life on Earth is powered by solar energy—energy in the form of light and heat that comes from the sun. We harness it into electric power. Because it comes from the sun, it is renewable. It isn't going to run out. Ice reflects this solar energy, while water and land absorb it, warming up the land and water.

The greenhouse effect traps energy on the earth, not allowing it to go back into the atmosphere. This effect is what keeps the earth's average climate the same, so that Earth is a

GREENHOUSE GASES
TRAP HEAT

comfortable place to live. The gases that keep us warm and maintain the greenhouse effect are called greenhouse gases.

But more greenhouse gases mean that more energy is trapped in the atmosphere. When additional gases are trapped, the temperature goes up, leading to climate change. We call it the greenhouse effect because it is like trapping solar energy in a greenhouse.

Earth's energy is usually in balance—the temperature of the earth does not change much, and the amount of energy leaving Earth is the same as the amount of energy reaching it from the sun.

Without the greenhouse effect, the surface temperature of the earth would be about 0 degrees Fahrenheit. Any water on the surface of the planet would freeze. No plants would be able to grow. Having the greenhouse effect at just the right level maintains life on Earth, as it has done for billions of years.

Carbon dioxide, or its chemical formula CO_2, is one

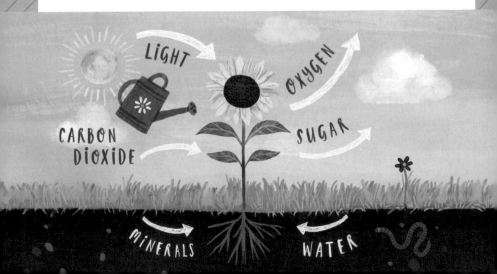

greenhouse gas. Humans and other animals release carbon dioxide when we exhale. The decomposition, or breaking down, of dead things produces methane, another kind of greenhouse gas. Volcanic eruptions have thrown many greenhouse gases into the atmosphere over time and some kinds of rocks have also released gases into the atmosphere. Things that produce greenhouse gases are called sources; some are natural sources. Natural sources are how greenhouse gases originally entered the atmosphere.

Plants absorb carbon dioxide through a process called photosynthesis when they make food, taking carbon dioxide out of the atmosphere. Algae in the ocean are also good at absorbing carbon dioxide, and seawater can absorb tons of carbon dioxide. Methane leaves the atmosphere naturally over decades. Things that remove greenhouse gases are called sinks.

Natural sinks can remove as many greenhouse gases as natural sources put into the atmosphere, so the amount of natural greenhouse gases stays roughly the same. This keeps greenhouse gas levels stable. The energy balance can change naturally, but over thousands of years. Unnatural sources of greenhouse gases, like human activity, can upset this balance rapidly and dangerously by increasing the strength of the greenhouse effect, changing the climate in just a few decades.

Carbon dioxide is the most abundant of the greenhouse gases and measuring it is a good way to measure the greenhouse effect as it changes naturally over time, allowing us to check on the temperature of Earth's atmosphere. Even little differences can have big consequences.

One thousand years ago, during Europe's medieval ages and the Islamic golden age, there were less greenhouse gas emissions, so there was less carbon dioxide in the atmosphere, and Earth's atmosphere wasn't as warm as it is today.

But during the times of the dinosaurs, carbon dioxide levels were higher, and

A representation of farming in the Middle Ages

Earth was much warmer, with jungles growing in what is now Canada and Russia. It took millions of years for the natural processes of Earth, such as oceans absorbing carbon dioxide, to lower carbon dioxide levels from dinosaur times to human times.

By studying chemicals left in rocks, ice, and sediment, or the mud at the bottom of the ocean, scientists can track historic gases and climates. Greenhouse gases are the strongest indicators of changes in the climate.

But now, instead of following natural processes like the oceans, humans have been adding tons of greenhouse gases to the atmosphere for the last two hundred years because we are burning fossil fuels that produce a lot of carbon dioxide. The climate is changing in just a few decades, faster than ever before.

But the greenhouse effect is just one part of understanding climate change.

CALL TO ACTION!

START A BIKE CLUB

One of the best ways for an individual to reduce the greenhouse gases they produce is to burn less fossil fuel, like gasoline. Riding a bicycle doesn't burn fossil fuels or produce greenhouse gases, so cycling instead of driving can reduce carbon emissions by a lot.

But not every city is bikeable. A great way to get more people to ride bikes is to make sure that cities have infrastructure such as bike lanes and bike parking. You can start a club at your school or in your community to encourage your city to install bike-friendly routes and dedicated parking. Because around 7 percent of green-house gases come from people driving cars, biking is one of the best ways to reduce this impact on climate change.

CHAPTER 3

FORCES OF THE EARTH

Everything on Earth is connected.

The major forces of Earth, or huge things that change the planet, like air and water, constantly interact and naturally change each other. But humans are also a changing force on the earth, and human-made climate change is one of the biggest unnatural changes to forces that we have ever seen.

Air, water, and land are three of the most fundamental

forces on Earth. Air includes the air we breathe and also air in our atmosphere that keeps Earth warm. Water includes all the fresh water on Earth, all the salt water in the ocean, all the ice at the north and south poles, and all the precipitation around the world. Land includes mountains, valleys, the tectonic plates that move the continents, and everything on the earth's crust.

Air moves water by turning it into clouds and rain and, as rain falls on land, it carries away tiny bits of rock in a process called erosion. Over a long time, erosion shapes land by carving valleys and breaking down mountains.

Life is also one of the most fundamental forces on Earth. Plants absorb water and also release water vapor into the air, which helps to control weather patterns. Animals dig into rocks, breaking up stone over time. Animals also produce methane and carbon dioxide, which enter the atmosphere. From the smallest bacterium to the biggest forest, life is always changing the earth.

All these different natural forces interact constantly in millions of ways, but unequal heating is the engine that drives them.

The equator is the warmest part of the earth because it is closest to the sun. The north and south poles are farther away from the sun's heat, so they are colder. This difference in temperature is called unequal heating. Earth rotates on an

axis, like a marshmallow on a stick, giving us night and day. Earth is also slightly tilted on its axis. The tilt of Earth's axis gives us seasons.

While the equator is always closer to the sun, the tilt means that the northern half of the earth, or the northern hemisphere, points just a little bit more toward the sun and receives more sunlight for half of the year. This time is what we call summer in the northern hemisphere.

In the other half of the year, the northern hemisphere points a little bit away from the sun and receives less sunlight, making it colder and causing what we call winter. The time in between pointing toward and away from the sun gives us spring and fall. The timing of the seasons is the opposite for the southern hemisphere.

Warm air rises and cold air falls. Because the air at the equator is always warmer than the rest of the earth, the air at the equator warms up and rises into the atmosphere. As it moves up, it eventually hits the tropopause, which is like the "roof" of the atmosphere. The warm air then spreads out like smoke inside a house.

This warm air pushes the air around it out of the way and leaves an empty space at the equator behind it. The warm air spreads out toward the poles, pushing more air out of the way and becoming cooler as it gets farther from the equator.

Eventually, this air loses the heat that kept it afloat and becomes cool enough that it falls back to the surface of Earth. Then, the cool air moves toward the equator, filling the empty space left behind by warm air. This causes air to circulate between the equator and the poles. As the air moves along the earth's surface back to the equator, it causes things like wind, which is moving air. This system is called atmospheric circulation.

As this wind crosses the earth it also moves water with it. Water naturally evaporates—the liquid water turns into a gas in the air called water vapor. Wind carries this water vapor around the earth with it as it goes, causing weather like rain. Clouds are made of water vapor, and rain happens when there is too much water vapor in the air for the air to hold it all. Atmospheric circulation caused by unequal heating moves air and water all over the earth and powers the weather.

Wind also pushes the surface of the ocean, making waves but also moving much more water below the surface of the ocean. Water moving below the surface is called an ocean current. This water moves to and from the equator through the oceans, bringing warmer water to colder places and colder water to warmer places.

Ocean currents move nutrients, or things that plants and animals feed on, around the ocean. The moving currents create important food sources for plants and animals around the world. This is another example of interactions between forces on Earth, and something that climate change alters. The climate of the earth changes the strength of atmospheric circulation, and changing the climate of the earth has serious consequences for the movement of air and water worldwide. Climate change affects weather patterns all over Earth.

There are countless other interactions between the forces. For instance, mountains may block wind, changing weather patterns and determining where plants can grow. Or humans may choose to avoid dry areas and live in the jungles, leaving one side of the mountains untouched but other sides covered in buildings full of technology.

Forces of nature can shape the world and change each other. Earth is a complex, delicate system. Small changes in one force alter other forces. Understanding even small inter-actions between forces on Earth is crucial to understanding our world and why climate change is so important; it is one of the biggest changes to these forces that we have ever seen.

But humans are also one of the biggest forces on Earth. From digging deep inside the earth, to catching fish out of the oceans, to emitting greenhouse gases that change the climate, humans are upsetting the delicate balance that holds the forces

of the earth together. Things humans do and changes humans make are called anthropogenic forces. Climate change is our biggest change to the earth, but it is far from our only one.

Humanity is witnessing how much power people now have to change the world around us. It is crucial to know what the world was like before we had this power so we know how different modern climate change is to everything that came before it.

Prehistoric Climates

It is also important to know what Earth looked like for the last several thousand years, before human beings first began to develop civilizations and technologies. Earth's average climate does change naturally. Massive volcanic eruptions can block out the sun, causing temperatures to drop. Or tectonic plates can shift, causing changes in the kinds of rocks that can absorb or release greenhouse gases over millions of years.

Natural changes usually happen on huge time scales, over thousands, tens of thousands, or millions of years. Ninety million years ago, when dinosaurs still walked, Earth was so warm that the north and south poles were covered with thick, humid forests, and the average global temperature was 80 degrees Fahrenheit. It was very different from the average 57 degrees Fahrenheit of today. But we can see natural changes more recently.

Twenty thousand years ago, glaciers, or giant sheets of ice, covered most of northern North America, southern South American, and northern Europe and Asia. Humans lived in Africa, Asia, and southern Europe. The planet was colder than it is now. Walls of ice 1 mile thick scraped over the land that is now New York City. Woolly mammoths, saber-toothed cats, and sloths the size of cars walked the earth. Vast grasslands and prairies covered most of the exposed land. The ocean was 300 feet lower than it is now. The average temperature on Earth was about 46 to 50 degrees Fahrenheit.

This may not seem like enough for glaciers to form everywhere, but it's important to remember that this is the average temperature; the northern parts of the world were much, much colder than that—cold enough that glaciers never melted, even in summer.

These enormous glaciers had existed for about one hundred thousand years, with even more glaciers growing and shrinking over millions of years before that. They carved out valleys and mountains and picked up millions of tons of rock and stone, pushing and pulling on the earth as they moved

Milutin Milanković

slowly across continents. But around twenty thousand years ago, the glaciers began to shrink for the last time.

Earth's orbit around the sun naturally changes very slowly every ten thousand or twenty thousand years. These changes are called Milankovitch cycles, named after their discoverer, Serbian scientist Milutin Milanković. The cycles slowly warm or cool Earth as the planet becomes closer to or farther from the sun. Scientists believe that a slight change in the orbit of Earth around the sun caused the glaciers covering parts of the planet to receive more sunlight and then start to melt, releasing carbon dioxide that had been trapped under the ice.

This carbon dioxide then started to heat the atmosphere, and little by little, the planet's temperature started to rise. The glaciers began a slow retreat to the north and south poles. Some scientists think this movement revealed enough land for humans to walk from Asia to North America on the Bering Land Bridge around twenty thousand years ago. This process would have taken thousands of years; climate change today is happening over decades.

The planet continued to warm, and the ice continued to

HOW DO WE KNOW?

We know about prehistoric climates because of a combination of many records left by natural processes on Earth. Sediment that formed in oceans, rivers, and lakes; chemical compounds and the gases in layers of ice inside remaining glaciers; rings that formed inside trees; and chemicals from the atmosphere in old coral reefs are all tools that scientists use to tell us about the climate before humans kept records.

melt. Eventually, forests took the place of grasslands. Water from the glaciers flowed into the oceans, raising Earth's sea level to where it is today. In time, the glaciers retreated entirely, leaving only remnants in the mountains of North America and Europe and the ice sheets that cover Antarctica. Woolly mammoths, along with many other Ice Age mammals, became extinct because their environment had changed. The temperature reached a peak of about 58 degrees Fahrenheit about ten thousand years ago, where it stayed for around eight thousand years, before beginning a slow decline.

Most of human civilization happened in that slow decline from 58 degrees Fahrenheit two thousand years ago to 56 degrees Fahrenheit in the late 1800s. The temperature has been remarkably stable for about the last ten thousand years. Before that, it took about ten thousand years to warm 8 degrees Fahrenheit across the planet. These are natural changes in climate that happen all the time.

But the climate change taking place now is different. In the early 2020s, the average global temperature of Earth is about 59 degrees Fahrenheit. This is 2 degrees Fahrenheit warmer than the temperature in 1960, and 3 degrees Fahrenheit warmer than temperatures in the 1800s, before the use of modern machinery.

CIRCUMPOLAR PEOPLES

Groups of people have lived around the north pole for thousands of years. The Aleut of Alaska, the Inuit of Canada and Greenland, and the Saami of Russia have lived with ice and glaciers for their entire cultural history. They understand the poles, how to navigate ice sheets, how to survive in frozen worlds and hunt below the ice, and how ice and glaciers have shaped the land.

Some indigenous tribes, such as the Tlingit and Tagish to the south, have stories thousands of years old describing how glaciers moved, carving mountains and rivers. They named places based on when and how they were carved from the ice. There is an immense amount of knowledge about ice and the history of Earth that has been passed down through generations of circumpolar peoples.

But as the climate changes, the ice that defines these peoples' cultures is melting. What they know about the world may be lost as the poles warm and glaciers disappear. For them, fighting climate change is as much about protecting their history as it is about protecting their homes.

Inuit women carrying a loaded qamutik (an Inuit sled for traveling on snow and ice), Pangnirtung, 1946

The planet is very big, and it takes an incredible amount of energy to warm or cool it. Whereas it once took ten thousand years to warm up the planet by 8 degrees Fahrenheit, the planet has warmed three whole degrees in around two hundred years, with most of that warming happening in the last seventy years.

The climate today is changing at a faster speed than ever before. For the first time, people are causing climate change.

Why the Climate Is Changing Now

We know that people are changing the climate by adding more greenhouse gases to the atmosphere. We know that the rate of temperature change is about forty times faster than

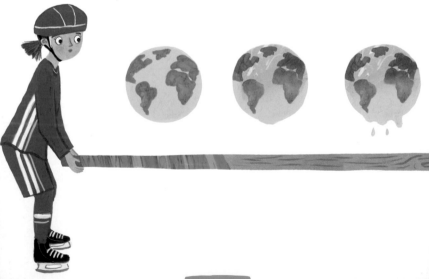

the rate over the last ten thousand years. We know that major changes to the earth in the last few centuries have been made by people. Modern climate change is not happening naturally.

If we plot the global temperature for the last two thousand years on a graph, it looks like a hockey stick. Temperatures for the last two thousand years are the long handle, with the short, sharp blade representing modern times. That sharp curve is the speed at which the climate is changing.

Very few natural things change the climate at this speed. Super volcanoes and meteors can cause the world's global temperature to drop by as much as 20 degrees Fahrenheit in a few months because of all the dust blocking out the sun, with consequences that can last for five years or even as long as centuries. However, there have not been any eruptions or meteor strikes in the last two centuries that would be big enough to cause the massive recent climate change, and those particular changes typically cool the earth, not warm it.

Earth could warm naturally if the sun suddenly became brighter or Earth's orbit became closer to the sun. The amount of energy from the sun plays a big role in controlling the overall temperature of Earth; more energy from the sun raises the temperature.

However, scientists have been monitoring changes in the sun for decades and there is no evidence that the sun is producing more energy to warm the earth. Also, the Milankovitch cycles, changes in the earth's orbit around the sun, occur on scales of thousands of years. In fact, scientists think that, if anything, Milankovitch cycles should be starting another ice age. But, instead, the planet is warming.

The only other real reason for the climate to change as it has been is the increase in greenhouse gases, and the only new sources of greenhouse gases in the last several centuries have been human ones. Scientists have measured the level of carbon dioxide in the atmosphere since 1958. Since then, the level of carbon dioxide in the atmosphere has only gone up.

Based on samples taken from the cores of glaciers and from sediment at the bottom of the ocean, we know that before humans began producing lots of greenhouse gases, carbon dioxide levels had been steady for about the last ten thousand years. Carbon dioxide levels in the atmosphere began to increase during the 1700s and 1800s, when humans first began burning fossil fuels on a huge scale, releasing carbon dioxide.

There are more carbon dioxide and other greenhouse gases in the atmosphere than there were two hundred years ago. These gases are caused by people and make the climate warmer.

CALL TO ACTION!

WORKING TOGETHER

Groups of people are more powerful than individuals working alone, so the most effective way to help bring attention to climate change is to organize a club with people who care about our climate and want to do things differently.

The club can be at your school or in your community. Talk to classmates, teachers, and adults about having time during the week for a meeting to talk about science and the environment. Then talk to people outside the group about climate change. Start a newspaper that you can distribute in your school and to the community through supermarkets, restaurants, coffee shops, and social events. Clubs can also plan community recycling events or other environmental activities.

ClimateTimes VOL.1

SAVE OUR EARTH

CHAPTER 4

FOSSIL FUELS

Everything people do has an impact on our environment.

Sometimes, these impacts are good—people plant trees that remove carbon dioxide from the atmosphere and reduce the power of climate change. But much of the time, human impacts produce new greenhouse gases that enter the atmosphere and make climate change worse. Everything in our homes was made by releasing carbon dioxide and other greenhouse gases into the atmosphere in some way. We know this because almost everything that keeps our world running today requires fossil fuels.

The fossil fuels coal, oil, and natural gas are fuel sources made of carbon that comes from the ground. Fossil fuels are the fuel for all our world's industry, agriculture, and transportation. They power everything, including our homes, cities,

schools, and hospitals. We also make essential materials like plastics out of fossil fuels.

Fossil fuels have allowed civilization to grow at an extremely rapid rate and have increased the quality of life for people all around the world. Fossil fuels have allowed us to move faster, have given us products such as air conditioning, and helped modern medicine with the mass production of medications and sterile tools. But the burning of fossil fuels releases carbon dioxide into the atmosphere, which means they are not only the fuel for our world's greatest achievements; they are also the fuel for our world's biggest problem: climate change.

The History of Fossil Fuels

Between about 1780 and 1850, cities in northern Europe and North America began to switch from wood as their primary source of fuel toward a new source of energy that had been discovered in vast quantities: coal. People have been using coal since before the Roman Empire, with ancient China possibly having a coal mine three thousand years ago. But for most of human history, wood was our primary source of heat.

The worldwide industrial revolution started around 1760 in England and is still happening today as developing countries start burning more fossil fuels than wood. But its beginning kickstarted a transition from civilizations that were mostly based around farms and producing just enough food to survive, toward civilizations that were based upon cities and their production of physical goods, like clothing or machinery. Suddenly, people went from mostly living in spread-out rural societies, mainly

Chinese coal miners in an illustration of the Tiangong Kaiwu Ming Dynasty in the seventeenth century.

farming, to a world where people flocked to cities to work in factories. Farming decreased while still producing enough food. This transition began in Europe and North America but spread to almost every other part of the globe.

WHAT ARE FOSSIL FUELS?

Fossil fuels are made from the bodies of plants and animals that died millions of years ago, but nearly all fossil fuels today are made of plant matter. Over three hundred million years ago, the earth was much warmer and wetter than it is today. Enormous jungles covered much of the planet and algae filled the oceans. When all those plants died, they were buried under layers of mud and sediment.

For millions of years, the buried plants had rock pressing down on them. This extreme heat and pressure caused the plants to undergo chemical reactions and turn into the fossil fuels that we use today.

We collect fossil fuels by digging them out of the ground in mines that travel deep underground, sucking them out of the earth with giant pumps, or using chemicals to turn carbon-rich sands and rocks into oil. The processes that formed coal, oil, and natural gas took millions of years to complete. Because we cannot make more fossil fuels in our lifetimes, fossil fuels are called nonrenewable resources, or resources that will eventually run out.

Fossil fuels became popular because they have a high energy density. This means that coal burns longer and hotter than any kind of wood, gasoline can power cars to run for miles on just one gallon of liquid, and natural gas is easy to store and produces more energy than either coal or oil. These fuels are easy to transport, they contain a lot of energy for little weight, and they were incredibly abundant when they were first discovered in the 1700s and 1800s. At the beginning of the industrial revolution, there was a lot of coal in the United Kingdom, much of which washed ashore. In the early 1900s, digging a single well in an oil-rich state like Texas or Oklahoma was enough to produce what seemed like an infinite supply of oil. Now, it is more difficult to find fossil fuels.

Wooden water wheel, 1915.

Because fossil fuels are so energy dense, come in liquid and gaseous forms, and were easily accessed in the past, they became essential to powering complicated machinery. Additionally, fossil fuels are more reliable than older forms of energy. Old wooden windmills and wooden water wheels were once common across Europe and other parts of the world. They used the power of wind and water to spin enormous stone wheels. Those wheels crushed crops into flour or powered the movement of machinery such as looms that produced fabric. Those power sources could not produce as much energy as fossil fuels, and they also did not work all the time, such as when the wind wasn't blowing. So people began to rely on fossil fuels to turn grindstones or do other tasks, because fossil fuels work on demand.

But burning fossil fuels releases carbon dioxide into the atmosphere. When we burn them, their carbon reacts with oxygen in the air to create carbon dioxide—the carbon dioxide that is making our planet warmer. All fossil fuels produce carbon dioxide. There is no way to use fossil fuels without creating carbon dioxide.

Because humans have been burning fossil fuels for hundreds of years, and because we use more and more fossil fuels every year, we are putting more and more carbon dioxide into the atmosphere every year. Carbon dioxide either stays in the atmosphere for centuries, or it is absorbed by water or plants, so all the carbon we've ever burned is now in the atmosphere, the ocean, or the trees.

Most of the carbon we've ever burned is in water and plants. About 50 percent of all human-produced greenhouse gases are absorbed by these natural carbon sinks that take the gases out of the atmosphere, reducing climate change. This is one reason trees are so important for stopping climate change.

However, this also means that 50 percent of all emissions are still in the atmosphere, causing direct climate change. To

make this worse, humans are cutting down trees to create more land for farming and to make furniture, so there are fewer plants to suck up carbon dioxide. That means there is more carbon dioxide going into the atmosphere.

It's no coincidence that carbon dioxide levels in the atmosphere began to increase around the same time that humans began burning huge amounts of fossil fuels. Carbon dioxide levels have been increasing for centuries, but they have increased the most since the mid-twentieth century. Fossil fuels are fueling climate change.

There are other problems with fossil fuels besides that they help cause climate change. For example, oil cannot be used in its raw form from the ground. It must be processed and turned into gasoline and plastics. The chemicals used to process oil are dangerous to people and animals. Some of the chemicals can cause cancer, breathing problems, and even nerve damage if people breathe them in or even just touch them. These chemicals or others like them are sometimes accidentally released into the environment, damaging all living things. Chemicals are released into the air as a side effect of burning some forms of oil. Coal also releases sulfur dioxide, a colorless gas, when it is burned. If it is raining when it is released, sulfur dioxide causes acid rain that can damage our lungs as well as harm our skin or even buildings.

Mining for fossil fuels is also dangerous to people and the environment. Much like oil refining, mining for coal uses chemicals that are harmful to living things. Miners can also breathe in smoke that causes lung diseases.

Once plentiful, people now need more extreme ways to

Sustainability is a way for humans to live in balance with nature, not destroy it, and to protect it for future generations. Burning fossil fuels is not sustainable; they will run out and they are damaging the environment.

get nonrenewable fossil fuels from the ground. One way is fracking, which uses high-pressure water power to break the ground and collect the oil. Scientists estimate that we have about fifty years of oil, fifty-two years of natural gas, and one hundred fourteen years of coal left. So these sources will run out; we will have to find a new source of energy on Earth.

Stopping the use of fossil fuels is the best solution to stop climate change but "best" does not mean "easiest."

Every country except for Iceland and Tajikistan gets most of its energy from fossil fuels. Electricity grids, power plants, cities, and homes are built and powered using fossil fuels. The only long-term solution is to switch to alternative fuel sources that are not based on fossil fuels and will not run out. These fuel sources are called renewable resources.

But building alternative sources of power is expensive for governments and takes time. Stopping fossil fuel use will also remove jobs, even though switching to renewable energy would create jobs. And unfortunately, even without fossil fuels, there are still other things that produce greenhouse gases.

RENEWABLE ENERGY

Renewable energies are sources of power that don't run out, instead capturing energy from the natural world to turn it into electricity. Power from the sun, the wind, and moving water are all examples of renewable energy. They are cheaper, more reliable, and more efficient than ever. Modern batteries store power for when the wind isn't blowing or the sun isn't shining. People can also enjoy the sun, wind, and water while they are being used as sources of renewable energy. Renewable energies are the best option for a future without fossil fuels.

Other Sources of Greenhouse Gases

Creating cement emits high amounts of carbon dioxide because cement has to be fired in a fossil-fueled oven, and making cement also causes chemical reactions that release carbon dioxide into the atmosphere. Some scientists estimate that creating cement is responsible for 5 to 8 percent of all carbon dioxide emissions worldwide. Cement is one of the most-used resources on the planet because it is strong and long-lasting. This is why it is used to build cities. The only resource used more is water.

Other sources of greenhouse gases are air conditioners and refrigerators. These cooling machines use chemicals called fluorinated gases that sometimes escape from old machines. Fluorinated gases only account for a small percentage of global greenhouse gas emissions but they are thousands of times more effective than carbon dioxide at trapping heat; they are a major threat to our climate.

Getting rid of these gases is difficult because there are not many alternatives. Fluorinated gases are themselves an alternative for older refrigerating chemicals that created a hole in the atmosphere, letting in harmful ultra-violet rays from the sun.

Almost everything on Earth gives off greenhouse gases in some way, through energy use, chemical reactions, or destroying forests that used to absorb carbon dioxide.

Transitioning the world away from fossil fuels is the most important way to fight climate change, though as with everything in climate change, there are no easy solutions. But solutions are possible.

CALL TO ACTION!

NEIGHBORHOOD ENERGY

Reducing energy usage is a great way to fight climate change, but using renewable energy to produce electricity is even better. Finding a way to get renewable energy for your home can be difficult, though. Some utility companies or private businesses offer options to buy electricity from renewable sources like wind and solar, and other companies can install solar panels on homes. However, not every region can do this, and, sometimes renewable energy options are expensive.

Neighborhood energy can be an answer. Start a campaign to get renewable energy to your neighborhood. People can contribute resources to buy solar panels or a wind turbine for the neighborhood, or they can work as a group to encourage utility companies to use more renewable energy. Working with neighbors is an effective way to change local energy sources.

CHAPTER 5

WhERE EMiSSiONS COME FROM

Greenhouse gases in the atmosphere are a kind of pollution, as is anything that is causing damage to our environment. There are different kinds of pollution: greenhouse gases, other chemicals, and manure on farms are all pollution but all have different effects. Pollution does not all come from the same place. Most scientists refer to greenhouse gases as emissions, or things that are released into our atmosphere, from cars for example. They do not usually refer to them as pollutants. Scientists use "pollution" to refer to other harmful things in the environment. Pollution is a separate problem but it is related to climate change.

One of the best ways to fight climate change is for everyone to understand where greenhouse gas emissions are coming from and try to get polluters to reduce the amount of carbon dioxide they create. Scientists know where greenhouse gases are coming from, but many people may not. Greenhouse gases come from a few different sources.

The largest source of greenhouse gases is in the production of energy, burning fossil fuels to make electricity. Energy

production creates about 55 percent of all greenhouse gas emissions on Earth. Everything uses energy to function, from factories to houses to the power plants themselves. This source contains so many smaller ones that it is easier to divide it into two smaller sources: industry and electricity production.

Most of the energy that is created, and therefore the biggest polluter, is used for industry. Mines, factories, steel mills, chemical plants, cement, and energy production itself use the most energy. The next largest energy polluter is the heating and cooling of buildings and the use of electric lights and computers, especially in cities where many people live and work.

The next biggest polluter is agriculture. Adding up every part of food production and farming, from the energy it takes to run farms and machinery to the burning of forests to create new farmland, agriculture generates about 25 percent of the world's greenhouse gases. The burning of forests releases carbon dioxide through smoke and also reduces the number of trees that act as sinks to collect the carbon dioxide. Just one part of agriculture, livestock—such as cows—produces 9 percent of the world's total greenhouse gases through methane gas.

The third-largest source of greenhouse gases is transportation.

Cars, planes, buses, and container ships all burn fossil fuels to produce the energy they need to move and are responsible for 15 percent of the world's total greenhouse gas emissions.

With 55 percent of emissions from energy, 25 percent from agriculture, and 15 percent from transportation, that leaves 5 percent of greenhouse gases unaccounted for. These extra emissions come from smaller sources, like the decomposition of waste in landfills, leaks in fossil fuel pipes, power plants that accidentally release greenhouse gases, and nuclear power, which needs fossil fuels to mine the elements in nuclear fuel.

The total: 100 percent of human-made greenhouse gases. But these sources are still broad, and they overlap. For

example, the greenhouse gas emissions from the transportation of food falls into both transportation and agriculture. Deciding

where greenhouse gas emissions come from can be very difficult, but because there are so many different sources, there are also many different ways to decrease those emissions, one source at a time.

Polluter Statistics

Knowing what produces greenhouse gases is important, and so is knowing where these greenhouse gases are produced, so global efforts can try to stop them. Different countries have different laws, governments, and societies that view greenhouse gases, industries, and fossil fuels differently. To reduce greenhouse gas emissions worldwide, it is important that countries work together.

In 2017, about 34.81 billion tons of carbon dioxide emissions were produced.

In 2020, China was the biggest producer of global greenhouse gas emissions, with 10.67 billion tons of carbon

dioxide. The United States produced the second most green-house gases at 4.71 billion tons, followed by India's 2.44 billion tons. The order of this ranking has been the same for about the last decade.

The countries that produce the least amount of green-house gases only produce about 0.01 percent of the amount produced by China. The least-producing countries are almost all island countries, and they have millions of inhabitants.

Dividing the amount of carbon dioxide produced by the population of a country shows a rough average of one person's impact on the environment. These are called per capita measurements. Remember that people use different amounts of resources and that governments and businesses make the decisions that result in global climate change, like deciding to use fossil fuels instead of renewable energy.

The average Chinese citizen produces 7.4 tons of carbon dioxide per person. The United States produces 14.24 tons per person. India only produces about 1.78 tons per person. Countries like Samoa and Rwanda are about 1.24 and 0.8 tons per person, respectively. United States citizens have, on average, a larger carbon footprint, or how much carbon they produce, than people in China or India because of the number of people in the United States.

Countries like Qatar, Kuwait, and Canada have very high greenhouse gas emissions compared to their smaller

populations, because they are large fossil fuel-producing countries.

But there is one more way to know which countries have contributed the most to climate change. China produces the most greenhouse gases today, but as a country, it has only been producing these high levels of emissions since about the 1990s. Not every country started their emissions at the same time.

Throughout China's history, it has contributed only about 12 percent of all greenhouse gas emissions. By contrast, the European Union, which produces just 7 percent of annual emissions now, is responsible for 22 percent of all human greenhouse gas emissions throughout history, because it polluted for much longer and more intensely in the past.

Even though greenhouse gas emissions from the United States are falling now, it is responsible for the most greenhouse gas emissions, producing 25 percent of all greenhouse gases.

Climate change is cumulative, and many countries have been responsible.

WHAT'S MY FOOTPRINT?

People talk about their carbon footprint. People in wealthier countries tend to use more resources because resources are more easily available. If everyone lived like the average American, we would need five Earths to supply enough resources for everyone.

While there are many ways that individuals can reduce their footprints, such as buying few products or driving less, these have little impact on climate change unless everyone changes.

It is important to be more sustainable in our everyday lives, but it is also important to know that the biggest and most effective ways to fight climate change come from groups of people working together to change all of society. Governments and businesses have the most say in the kinds of resources that are used and how they are used.

CALL TO ACTION!

ZERO AND THE FOUR RS

You can start a Zero Club to encourage people to strive for zero greenhouse gases by using less things that produce them.

Your club can use the four Rs: refuse, reduce, reuse, and recycle. If you don't need something, refuse it. If you need something, reduce how much you use. Try to reuse items instead of buying new. Recycle when possible. Getting people to practice the four Rs can turn individual actions into group actions.

REFUSE · REDUCE · REUSE · RECYCLE

CHAPTER 6

LONG-TERM EFFECTS

It's important to know what causes climate change and who is causing it so we can make changes.

Climate change is making the earth unstable and changing how we all interact. The climate that humans have been used to for the past ten thousand years is no longer something we can rely on.

Scientists have limited data to understand how the earth

is going to change but they know it is changing. Even the most optimistic predictions of climate change's effects are scary.

The biggest effect of climate change—the overall temperature of the earth—will continue to increase.

Sea levels rise as the earth warms, and the ice trapped in glaciers in the north and south poles melts, adding water to the oceans. This is already causing coastal flooding, and it will get worse.

Coastal cities are at risk. Sea levels may rise 1 foot or as much as 8 feet by 2100.

The amount of fresh water will decrease. As the planet warms, warmer air causes places to become drier. Most places around the world will have higher heat and less water.

Droughts prevent farms from getting enough water. Crops die and there may not be enough food for everyone. Heat waves are more common. Heat waves are among the most dangerous weather events; people without air conditioning might die from being too hot. Many countries in the world do not have air conditioning because they never needed it before. Heat waves and droughts also lead to larger and stronger wildfires.

Storms are already getting more intense. Hurricanes are powered by warm water, and warmer oceans from climate change mean stronger storms. Storms also happen more frequently and in new places. This, combined with higher sea levels, makes coastal regions more dangerous places. Billions of people live on coasts; coastal flooding is a major threat to lives and livelihoods. The Maldives is building new islands that are three feet taller than its existing islands, so that it can withstand sea level rise and stronger storms.

A combination of all these effects will force many people to move, seeking more stable places to live. People escaping the effects of climate change are called climate refugees or climate migrants. People who live around Lake Chad in Northern Africa, which has lost 90 percent of its water area, are already looking for new places to live. Scientists predict that most climate refugees will be from low-lying island countries, and countries with fewer resources in South America, sub-Saharan Africa, and South Asia.

In the most optimistic outcome, food is a little harder to grow and low-lying island countries adapt to rising seas. More people move to cities, and droughts are more common but not devastating. Winters are shorter, and summers are hotter.

In the worst-case scenarios, cities can't manage the strong storms and flooded coasts. Deserts take over what was once farmland. People are forced toward isolated places nearer to the earth's poles.

The most likely outcome will be somewhere between these two options.

Scientists predict that many of these effects will be commonplace by the year 2100 or sooner if we do not act now. Burning fossil fuels and destroying forests has led to global climate change, but there is more than just climate change to worry about.

The Costs of Expansion

Every human action that contributes to climate change has other consequences beyond producing more greenhouse gases. Agriculture, mining, and building cities are all activities that contribute to climate change, but they also destroy natural habitats like forests and prairies that are home to thousands of

NI-VANUATU

The Ni-Vanuatu people in the Pacific islands migrated there over hundreds of years. People relied largely on yams, which are root vegetables, fish, and plants foraged from jungles. Kava, a drink made from plants only found on the Pacific islands, is central to many of the cultures. Creating instruments from island plants that represent the sounds of their ancestors during ceremonies is also an important part of the islanders' cultures.

The United Nations has listed Vanuatu as having the highest risk of natural disaster in the next several decades. Because of increasing storms, rising seas, and the risk of floods, the island nations are increasingly vulnerable to destruction from climate change. Indigenous peoples risk losing their homes and lifestyles.

A women's dance from Vanuatu, using bamboo stamping tubes.

different plants and animals. Pollution from factories, farms, and cities is being dumped into oceans, where it kills coral reefs, kelp forests, fish, and ocean mammals.

This destruction causes a huge loss in biodiversity, or the number of different species that exist in one place. This means that billions of animals are dying every year, damaging habitats that provide ecosystem services. Ecosystems are places where plants and animals live, but the term "ecosystem" also includes the climate, geography, and weather of a place. It describes everything about an animal's habitat. Ecosystem services are benefits to people that are provided by the ecosystems.

Perhaps the most important ecosystem service is the one that trees and grasses provide by absorbing carbon dioxide.

Forests along rivers and coasts also filter water by taking out chemicals, making the water usable by people.

Forests help stop floods by soaking up extra water. The trees stop soil erosion by holding soil in place with their roots. Soil erosion is when healthy soil gets washed away by wind or rain.

Ecosystems also soak up other pollutants, such as by taking smog out of the air, making it cleaner.

Keeping ecosystems healthy is essential for future generations of people.

Climate change shows us how everything in the world

interacts with everything else, and how actions can cause changes that are both good and bad. The burning of fossil fuels have helped civilizations grow but have also led to climate change; good, and bad.

There are no easy solutions. But there are solutions, from alternative energy, to rebuilding damaged ecosystems, to changing lifestyles. We need to act on them.

CALL TO ACTION!

YOUR SCHOOL, YOUR TOWN

Older towns and communities may rely heavily on fossil fuels or old technology that is bad for the earth. Older buildings like your school, a town hall, or a library may need extra energy to stay warm in winter or cool in summer. Work with your school and community to update older buildings so they are more sustainable.

Start a club to learn how much energy your school uses. You can campaign with classmates for your school district to install solar panels on the roof or even build a new, climate-friendly school. Talk to town governments about updating public buildings with low-energy electronics, using solar panels and wind turbines, purchasing energy from renewable sources, and buying electric vehicles for government services. Your school can help raise money to make these changes.

CHAPTER 7

AGGRAVATED AGRICULTURE

What did you eat for breakfast today? Where did that food come from? Perhaps you helped pick out the cereal at the grocery store, or maybe the eggs and bread were delivered to your home. Obviously, though, this food came from somewhere else before the grocery store or the van that brought it to you. It may have come from a warehouse or a ship that carried it across the ocean. But even before that, it came from agriculture.

Modern agriculture is one of the most interesting and important aspects of our world. Every living thing needs food. Most humans get their food from agriculture. With around eight billion people on Earth today, we would not be able to feed everyone without the advanced technologies available to farmers. But that ability to produce enough food comes with a dark side. Agriculture is one of the most environmentally destructive activities on Earth, producing more than one quarter of humanity's greenhouse gas emissions every year and accelerating climate change. But not only is agriculture polluting our atmosphere—it is also causing damage to the land.

Stopping this agricultural damage is a problem, because agriculture is the most crucial industry for human survival. Everyone has to eat, regardless of who they are or where they live. Finding ways to fix the problems with agriculture also involves understanding how this problem has happened.

The history of agriculture is complicated. Farming has got better at producing more food as farmers and scientists try to meet the needs of feeding more people. Farming gets more efficient, more people are born, and more land is needed to farm; it's a continuing cycle.

Sometimes, though, there isn't enough land available to farm. When this happens, farming is a race to produce more food with less space. Sometimes this works, so there is enough

WHY DO PEOPLE GO HUNGRY?

....

Some people cannot access food easily because of poverty or war or because their farms were wiped out by natural disasters. This has been true for thousands of years, but now we can grow enough food to feed everyone. The problem is that all the food cannot get to everyone in need. As climate change makes natural disasters worse, some countries are already starting to have their harvests wiped out. Preparing for climate disasters is more important than ever. Food is not equally shared among all countries and all peoples—this is the main reason why people go hungry.

food for everyone. When it doesn't work, there aren't enough crops to feed everyone. People go hungry. The single biggest reason that more people haven't gone hungry is the Green Revolution, or the use of modern technology to greatly improve the amount of food people can produce. Because we can grow more food, food becomes cheaper, and more people can access it more easily.

Overall, modern technology has found ways to produce more food for more people. The Green Revolution is the most recent example of agriculture's ability to keep up with a demand for food. It represents one of the biggest changes in farming since the birth of agriculture thousands of years ago.

In the 1960s, scientists and politicians began developing tools to increase food production without increasing land use. These tools included mechanized planting and harvesting of crops to reduce waste. One example is the use of tractors instead of horses to plow fields. Another is using metal harvesters to collect crops instead of collecting them by hand. These tools let farmers fit more crops into a field, increasing what they could harvest from a piece of land. These tools also include growing new, higher-yield varieties of crops that produce more food than older kinds of crops. Another tool is using high levels of powerful chemical fertilizers, or substances that were made in a factory to help plants grow, instead of natural substances that came from the earth. When combined, these tools have produced enough food to feed billions of people, reduce global poverty, use less land, and decrease greenhouse gas emissions by using less energy than growing the same

amount of food with old tools.

Modern agriculture has allowed people to avoid starvation and increase the quality of life for people by providing more access to more food. Ever since populations began to increase in the last three hundred years because of modern medicine and sanitation, there have been fears from small groups of scientists that population growth would eventually overtake food production. The most famous of these was Thomas Malthus, who predicted in the eighteenth century that the world would enter a stage of mass starvation in the nineteenth century. These fears have existed for over two hundred years, but they have never proven true. But scientists today believe that food production will have to increase by 60 percent to support Earth's population by 2050 unless people change their diets to more plant-based foods and we are more careful about how we grow our food.

Thomas Malthus

Modern agriculture also has many downsides, the biggest one being climate change. Agriculture, from running chicken farms to planting seeds and everything in between, is responsible for 25 percent of all greenhouse gas emissions. Machines like tractors burn fossil fuels, releasing greenhouse gases. Livestock like cows and pigs produce the greenhouse gas methane and are responsible for 6 percent of greenhouse gases. Fertilizers used on soil release nitrous oxides, another greenhouse gas, representing 4 percent of all greenhouse gases. Countries like India, which may choose to use cheaper, traditional farming methods, also have to burn crops to clear fields; burning these crops releases 4 percent of greenhouse gas emissions yearly. Deforestation contributes 8 percent of yearly greenhouse gas emissions, because burning forests releases carbon dioxide. And rice farming produces about 1.5 percent of greenhouse gases, because rice paddies release methane as they grow.

Tools like tractors destroy topsoil, the part of the soil that grows plants. This contributes to soil erosion, or the loss of healthy soil, worldwide. Chemical fertilizers add huge amounts of greenhouse gases to the atmosphere. These fertilizers, along with waste from livestock, also release water pollution that causes eutrophication, or an overgrowth of algae in water, leading to the death of fish in global lakes, rivers, and oceans. Pesticides kill millions of animals every year, reducing biodiversity in ecosystems. This has led to the global decline in bees.

Some places still rely on old technologies, making it harder for them to grow food. Some countries are burning down millions of acres of forest to get more land for agriculture, destroying homes for wildlife, and killing trees that help fight climate change.

Even though modern agriculture can get more food from less land, agriculture still uses millions of square miles of land, about 50 percent of all available land, not including deserts or ice. It also needs most of the freshwater that people use, and is a main reason for deforestation.

Modern agriculture may solve old problems but it causes new ones—not just how food is made but also what food we choose to make.

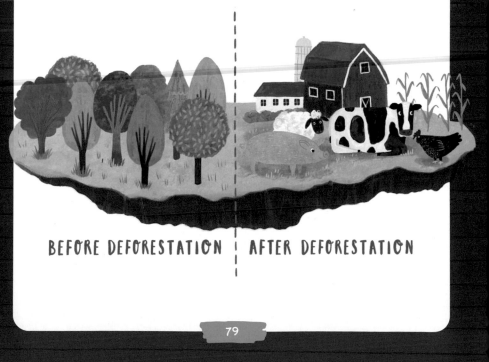

BEFORE DEFORESTATION   AFTER DEFORESTATION

A Day in the Life of a Steak

Beef steaks are symbols of progress. Once, only very wealthy people could afford to eat steak. Now, almost anyone can buy an affordable cut of steak. But that steak has a lot of hidden costs that aren't paid for with money.

There are two ways to raise cows. One is the pasture-grazing method, which is how cowboys did it in the early days of the west. This way, cows are raised in herds that wander over open fields, eating grasses and other plants. They do not need to be fed corn or given water because they get it from their pastures. They grow more slowly, their meat is more expensive, and they take up a lot of land, but they produce less water pollution and less greenhouse gases than the other method of raising cows.

That other method is a concentrated animal feeding operation (CAFO), also called a factory farm. In some CAFOs,

calves are put into single stalls or troughs in a tightly packed building. They are fed corn and soy, instead of their natural diet of grasses, so that they grow faster. Corn is high in carbohydrates, which increases fat, and soy is high in protein, which increases muscle. Growth hormones may be added to their diets to encourage even faster growth.

CAFO-raised cows produce more methane than pasture-raised cows.

These different approaches each have benefits and drawbacks. Pasture-raised cows have more space and are supposed to produce higher-quality meat, but this method requires huge tracts of land that could be used for prairie or forests. These prairies and forests could suck up carbon dioxide from the atmosphere, provide ecosystem services such as the filtering of water, and provide homes for hundreds of different species of animals.

Factory-farmed cows grow much faster, produce more meat that is less expensive, and don't need a lot of land to roam. In terms of land use and the amount of meat that gets produced, factory-farmed cows are better for the environment than pasture-raised cattle. But they also require tons of animal feed that takes up land to grow. For every 1 pound of beef produced, between 3 and 6 pounds of corn or soy also must be grown and fed to each cow. This uses up other land and resources like water.

All cows produce manure and methane, but factory-farmed cows produce a lot more. When there's a lot of manure in one place, it is full of dangerous bacteria and dangerously high levels of nutrients. This manure can enter waterways, such as rivers, lakes, or groundwater, polluting them and

leading to eutrophication. Eutrophication is caused by an overload of nutrients, when too many algae are in the water and the lack of oxygen kills fish and insects. This also causes waterways to turn bright green or bright red with algae. And methane traps heat in the atmosphere.

A life-cycle assessment means looking at the entire process of making something, from beginning to end. Regardless of whether a cow was pasture-raised or factory-farmed, it ends up as individual steaks packaged with plastic wrap, Styrofoam, or paper. These packaging materials also release greenhouse gases when they are made.

And the packaged meat still has to get to a grocery store. It may travel a thousand miles, sometimes even crossing oceans. The trucks and boats also produce greenhouse gases, and so do the refrigeration systems needed to keep the beef safe to eat. Refrigeration continues at the store where the steak is sold—more greenhouse gases. All this happens before anyone buys the steak.

These are some of the hidden costs of food. They aren't all financial costs. Beef has many hidden costs, like the land it takes to raise cattle or the water that is polluted by their waste, but every piece of food that gets consumed has its own hidden costs. Every piece of food sold at the grocery store is the final product of a process that requires water, energy produced by burning fossil fuels, land, machinery, time, and people. This is why agriculture takes up so much land and produces so many greenhouse gases.

Unequal Impacts of Food

The key here is that all agriculture has environmental impacts that contribute to climate change. Livestock has the single biggest impact on climate change, producing 6 percent of total greenhouse gases. But even foods like rice have impacts;

rice contributes about 1.5 percent of all greenhouse gases by releasing methane as it grows. But agriculture also uses immense amounts of land and water resources, taking those resources away from natural areas.

It may seem overwhelming to consider every aspect of these impacts, and it may seem like the challenge is impossible to overcome. Agriculture is always going to have an impact, whether it is taking up land that could be used for something else or taking water out of a river to grow corn instead of leaving the water in the river for natural ecosystems.

But we can change the impact of agriculture on the environment dramatically by changing what we grow, because all foods have different kinds of impacts and require different resources. Think of this like a footprint. Usually, a child's foot is smaller than an adult's foot. If a child steps in a patch of mud and the adult steps right next to them, there would be two footprints in the mud. They are both footprints, but they are not equal. This is also true of food. Two types of food may both be things you can eat, but they may have very different footprints.

Finding ways to change what we eat is one of the best ways

to reduce agriculture's impact on the environment. While reducing beef is one of the most effective ways to reduce the impact of farming, it isn't the only way. Reducing other kinds of meat consumption can help. So can purchasing foods that are grown sustainably, or without doing damage to the earth.

One Pound of Beef

Which weighs more: a pound of bricks or a pound of feathers? Of course, they weigh the same, but you need a lot more feathers than bricks to get one pound of feathers. We can apply an idea like this to food. One pound of beef weighs the same as one pound of nuts, but the resources that went into making one pound of either item are not the same. The exact weight of our samples doesn't matter. The easiest way to understand the different impacts of food is through examples.

The life cycle of factory-farmed beef is one good example. Between growing feed crops, raising cows, and shipping meat to stores, beef produces the most greenhouse gases of any food product. This is more than double the next biggest polluter, dark chocolate. Chicken, on the other hand, produces a smaller amount of gases, and tofu generates even less. The smallest producers are citrus fruits, nuts, and root vegetables like potatoes and yams.

Changing the kinds of foods we eat can increase or decrease the impact that farming has on our environment. Switching our diets from high-impact foods to low-impact foods leads to less fossil fuel energy being used to power the farms, water, and land. This produces less greenhouse gas, and therefore does less damage to the environment.

Not every impact is equal, even among food. Food impacts the environment in ways other than greenhouse gases. Water is one example. Cows drink water, water is used to grow corn for cows to eat, and water is used to package and transport beef. Most of the water used to produce beef is used to grow the corn to feed the cattle. If you combine all that water, 1 pound of beef uses roughly 325 gallons of water. This is the same as about how much water one adult should drink in one year. To understand how much water that is, 325 gallons of water weighs almost 2,700 pounds, or the weight of a small car. That's a lot of water!

But compared to other products, beef does not use the most water. One pound of cheese requires more than double the amount of water as beef. Nuts are among the lowest producers of greenhouse gases, but they are the second-highest user of water, after cheese. Somewhere in the middle is chicken. Onions use one of the least amounts of water.

Lamb requires more land than beef. Both animals use about the same floor space as a large apartment. Nuts and

tofu use very little land. The lowest land usage is by root vegetables.

The important point is that the total greenhouse gas emissions used to grow livestock, fish, and the crops the livestock eat account for 53 percent of all agricultural greenhouse gas emissions. But growing crops for human use, or crops like rice, potatoes, and nuts that are fed directly to people instead of livestock, generates only 29 percent of total greenhouse gas emissions.

Two-thirds of all crops are grown for direct human use, and only one-third are grown for livestock, but over half of all agricultural greenhouse gas emissions come from livestock and the crops used for raising them. Livestock and their feed crops use 75 percent of all agricultural land, whereas crops for human use only take up 25 percent of all agricultural land.

If we reduce the number of livestock that need food, we can reduce the number of crops we need to grow in order to feed them and free up land for forests.

Currently, the world is fed by using around 19 million square miles, though this is growing constantly and includes a lot of livestock. People who study agriculture think that if everyone on the planet had a vegan diet, or one that does not include any sort of animal product, we would reduce the amount of land needed for agriculture to around 4 million

square miles. If everyone on the planet had a vegetarian diet, or one that does not include meat, agricultural land could be reduced to around 8 million square miles.

This would free up land for natural ecosystems. Switching to either a vegan or vegetarian diet would also cut the amount of greenhouse gases and water pollution that livestock produce.

Of course, it is extremely unlikely that everyone in the world would switch to a vegan diet. Cutting out this much meat would also mean that many people who look after livestock and animal products would lose their jobs. The question is what kind of trade-offs we are willing to make to fight climate change.

We cannot and should not stop growing food. But we can change what we eat and how we grow it. One of the ways we can change how we grow food is by changing where we grow it.

Changing World, Changing Food

As the climate warms and changes, and the unstable weather of climate change becomes more common, scientists predict that events like floods and heat waves will become annual occurrences, and things once easy to find, like healthy soil and good farmland, will be more difficult to find. Floods and heat waves are already happening.

Farmers, scientists, and people who like cooking have been developing low-impact alternatives to high-impact goods for the last sixty years. These alternatives, high-protein plant-based foods like tofu, are now common. They use only a fraction of the land and produce a fraction of the greenhouse gases needed to produce meat. If more people choose to eat these low-impact alternatives, agriculture would spend less resources on livestock products and produce fewer greenhouse gases, easing climate change.

Scientists are also finding ways to grow real meat without the animal. Lab-grown meats might become another product on store shelves by 2030. These meats are the same as meat from animals, except lab-grown meats were never part of the animal. Scientists say that lab-grown meats will taste and feel just like real meat without needing huge amounts of water, land, or crops to produce them.

FOODS OF THE FUTURE

Other foods that may be more common include mushrooms, which are low-resource and high in nutrients, or kelp, which is a common part of some diets already. Insects, already eaten in some parts of the world, could become a main ingredient of foods too.

There are no easy solutions. Any kind of solution, or even a combination of several options, will have far-reaching consequences that can affect people in unexpected ways, and it is crucial that problems like job losses are not overlooked. But there are still steps we can take to stop climate change and every other problem that comes with it.

Eating less meat and other resource-intensive foods is one of the best ways to help agriculture reduce its damage to the environment, but practicing sustainable agriculture methods or buying products that are grown with sustainable agriculture methods are also great ways to help the earth and to fight climate change.

Sustainable agriculture does less damage to the environment and creates fewer greenhouse gases. Some sustainable farming methods are high-tech, but others are easy to implement with the right knowledge. There are many kinds of sustainable agriculture methods.

Low-tillage farming: When farmers plow their fields, a lot of soil is lost to wind and water. By tilling soil less, farmers can keep the soil healthier, saving soil and using fewer fertilizers that contribute to climate change.

Integrated pest management: Chemical pesticides kill pests, but they also kill bees and other helpful insects. By using other forms of pest control, like traps, plastic barriers, and predators like spiders, farmers can use fewer chemical pesticides.

Drip irrigation: Spraying entire fields with water results in a lot of that water being lost to evaporation, taking it out of the ground and away from people and natural areas. But by using small pipes full of holes, called drip irrigators, farmers can water plants exactly as much as they need, reducing the waste of water.

Cover crops: Instead of leaving fields empty after harvest, farmers can plant crops like winter wheat that keep the soil healthy and prevent erosion.

Urban farming: Growing plants in cities uses a lot of energy but makes it easy to farm all year and keeps out pests, using less land and producing more food.

There are dozens of other ways that farmers can improve farming methods. Eating fewer resource-heavy foods is not enough to solve all the problems. But with everyone working together to be sustainable, a better future for agriculture is within reach.

CALL TO ACTION!

FOOD AWARENESS

There are many hidden costs to food and there is a reason why they are called "hidden costs."

Stores do not usually tell people where food comes from, how much water it used, or what kind of greenhouse gas emissions it has produced. Together with a group of classmates, teachers, and other adults, you can raise awareness about food by showing people how many resources are used to produce the things we eat. This can encourage your neighbors, classmates, and towns to be aware about the food we eat, making them more likely to buy food that is better for the environment. The more people who make Earth-friendly purchases, the more likely that companies will want to make their businesses more sustainable. The more people who know and work together to change their diets to be more Earth-friendly, the bigger impact those dietary changes will have.

CALL TO ACTION!

SUSTAINABLE FARMING NEEDS YOU

There are many ways that farmers can help reduce their impact on the environment without losing their income. You can form a group or club at school to learn more about farming in and around your community, and what kinds of sustainable practices might already be in use. You can take field trips to farms. Your club can advocate, or encourage, sustainable farming.

Meet with local farmers, government officials, food distributors, and anyone who can encourage sustainable farming practices such as no-till farming, drip irrigation, integrated pest management, or cover crops.

Campaign for local governments to create sustainable farming programs in your city, county, or state. Your group could campaign for your town to start its own farm, where people can work together to grow food sustainably for the community.

CHAPTER 8

DEFORESTATION

Deforestation is a source of greenhouse emissions, and it is also made worse by the burning of fossil fuels.

Imagine that you're walking through the Cardamom Mountains rain forest in Cambodia. The air is hot and steamy from all the moisture. Thick vines hang from branches above you, and in the distance an elephant is trumpeting and stomping.

Some of the trees are hundreds of feet tall and many shades of green, with dozens of different species all around. These trees suck up carbon dioxide through photosynthesis, fighting climate change. You feel the bark of one tree. It's smooth, covered in marks from years of sun bears and elephants marking their territory.

You look up. High above you is the forest canopy, full of plants and animals, including some that never touch the ground. Clouded leopards, owls that swoop down to catch fish, and flowers that bloom on the branches of trees—the number of living things is dizzying.

With a roar, you're brought back to the ground by the sound of heavy machinery. You push aside leaves to find a field with stumps of trees scattered and burning. Giant bulldozers trundle across the field, crushing fallen logs and plants beneath their treads. Men with huge machetes hack away at the edges of the forest, cutting it back. Where there was once a forest teeming with life, there is now a smoldering ruin.

This deforestation is the Cardamom Mountains rain forest's reality. It is also reality for many other forests around the world that are being cut down and turned into farmland. Deforestation removes and burns trees, releasing back into the atmosphere all the carbon dioxide they had stored, making climate change worse.

Only about 13 percent of deforestation is done for lumber and to turn wood into paper. The rest is driven by an expansion of agriculture—to raise cattle and grow soybeans and palms for vegetable oil, which are used in both food and industry worldwide, and to grow other agricultural products, like rice and corn. Whatever the reason for deforestation, the result is the same: burning forests and hurting the earth.

The forests being destroyed contain thousands of species of plants and animals. They provide ecosystem services that keep millions of acres of soil from eroding with their roots, that help purify water by absorbing dangerous chemicals, and that suck up millions of pounds of greenhouse gasses from the atmosphere every year.

Millions of acres of these forests are cut down yearly, and much of this deforestation is concentrated in two regions: Brazil and Indonesia. These two countries account for half of all global tropical deforestation. The rest occurs in other tropical regions such as the Congo Basin, Nigeria, Honduras, the Philippines, and Cambodia. In Brazil, deforestation is mostly for beef. In Indonesia, it is typically for palm oil.

Brazil's Deforestation Problem

In the early 2000s, Brazil was suffering around 10,000 square miles of deforestation every year. That's more area than the entire country of El Salvador, every year. This was initially driven by Brazil's effort to produce more soy. After international regulations forced Brazil to stop deforestation for soy in around 2006, deforestation dropped dramatically.

There is debate about which year Brazil had its lowest deforestation but it was sometime between 2009 and 2021, with less than 2,000 squares miles of forest lost every year. Brazilian laws cut back on legal deforestation and gave extra resources to the Brazilian military to stop illegal deforestation. Illegal deforestation was one of the biggest causes of deforestation in Brazil.

Since about 2015, the Brazilian government has been less

attentive in enforcing restrictions on deforestation. As a way to develop its available resources, Brazil has been reducing environmental protections for the Amazon rain forest and resources for stopping illegal deforestation, which is usually carried out by poor people who feel they have no other choice. But now, instead of growing soy, the forest is being burned to create space for cattle and other livestock.

2000 ←——————————→ 2021

DEFORESTATION

2016 saw a sudden spike in deforestation, with around 22,394 square miles lost. 2021 saw the highest rates of deforestation in over twelve years, at around 7,500 square miles of forest lost. This is especially difficult for native peoples who live in the Amazon rain forest.

The native tribes of the Amazon rain forest have lived and worked in the forest ecosystem for thousands of years. Over that time, they have practiced and developed a lifestyle that allows them to sustain themselves through healthy ecosystems. Using techniques and knowledge learned over hundreds of generations they farm, fish, hunt, and gather plants from the Amazon, while still making sure that those resources will be available for future generations.

For example, some indigenous peoples of the Amazon have small farms that they move over time to allow the forest to regrow. Other indigenous peoples fish in the Amazon river when it floods its banks, catching the fish to eat and sell. The indigenous peoples know from their cultures how to make sure that their ecosystem remains stable. Because their lifestyles are dependent on healthy forests, the peoples work to protect and conserve the forests.

Scientists estimate that about 20 percent of the world's land is already protected by indigenous peoples, even though they make up only 5 percent of the world's populations. Scientists classify much of the lands inhabited by native

peoples as being in at least good ecological condition, and these places are losing animals and plants more slowly than most of the rest of the world. It is crucial to conservation efforts worldwide to recognize that indigenous peoples are already conserving the lands they call home, that they have a deep cultural knowledge of these lands, and that ecosystems can still be healthy and diverse with people living in them.

But cutting down the forests is making it impossible for indigenous peoples to protect these lands, because there are less lands to protect.

View of achiote flowers, seed pods, and leaves. The seed of the achiote plant is used to improve digestion, help manage diabetes, strengthen healthy bones, and reduce signs of aging.

When people cut down the Amazon rain forest, they are removing valuable resources such as medicinal plants and fruits that native people need to survive. Because deforestation and agriculture take up space that used to be forest, native people have to leave their homes and move to other parts of the forest.

Indigenous peoples

THE PEOPLE OF THE AMAZON RAIN FOREST

....

The Amazon rain forest expands beyond Brazil and has been home to hundreds of different cultures of native peoples, including the Awa, Waorani, Wajapi, and Yanomamo, for thousands of years. Some are nomadic hunter-gatherer groups who know when to move to a new area so that the jungle can regrow. Some build towns on stilts to live with the flooding of the Amazon basin. Today, many indigenous peoples worldwide participate in regional trade and incorporate modern technology into their lifestyles.

However, their territories are under attack from loggers and miners, who have been known to attack indigenous peoples who interfere with deforestation.

Village built on stilts along west bank of Rio Napo in Peru, a few miles above where it joins with the Amazon River. The land visible beyond the waterway is an island in the river.

all over the world have been dealing with land destruction for decades. In many countries, these people have a legal right to protect their land and homes, but some people cutting down the rain forests may not follow the laws, or in countries like Brazil, the laws are changed so native peoples no longer have the rights to their homes.

The homes of indigenous peoples worldwide are at risk from deforestation, agriculture, cities, and climate change, but the Amazon is just one place where this is happening.

The Complex Case of Palm Oil

On the equatorial Indonesian islands of Borneo, Sumatra, and Sulawesi, one of the leading causes of deforestation is the expansion of soybean and palm oil farms to make vegetable oil. Vegetable oil is a thick, clear liquid used in hundreds of products, including cookies, butter, makeup, industrial lubricants, and soap, and in industrial systems where it is a biofuel, or a fuel made from plants.

Palm oil, along with soybean oil, is one of the most common kinds of vegetable oils used worldwide and is crucial for businesses. Palm oil plantations in southeast Asia are responsible not just for deforestation but also for the death of more than a hundred thousand orangutans.

Orangutans are large, peaceful, intelligent apes that live on the islands in and around Indonesia. They have similar intelligence levels to human toddlers. Many people are afraid of orangutans because the apes are very large and can move quickly. But orangutans are critically endangered and nearing extinction. Scientists estimate there are about 100,000 orangutans left on Borneo, but there may be as few as 50,000 by 2025.

When people deforest the land to build palm oil plantations, they use huge machines, loud chainsaws, and blazing fires. This deforestation destroys orangutan habitats, causing the apes to run into fields, where they are frightened, confused, and homeless. These lost apes either die from having nowhere to go or are killed by the people planting the oil farms. Farmers sometimes kill orangutans because the apes can damage young palms by bending them to eat the fruit.

The easy solution would be to stop growing palms for palm oil and end the deforestation in Indonesia, but the answer is more complicated. Stopping Indonesian deforestation would help orangutans, help trees take carbon dioxide out of the atmosphere, and help the indigenous peoples who also make their homes in the forests, but palm oil makes up about 36 percent of the world's vegetable oil production, despite only using 9 percent of the world's vegetable oil land. So if palm oil production were stopped, it would save 9 percent of the total land used for vegetable oil, but the world would lose one-third of its total vegetable oil production. This would cause economic chaos in Indonesia and damage industry and food production worldwide.

Palm oil is like a super-producer of vegetable oil; palm oil trees can produce 50 percent more vegetable oil than soybeans, but only need about a quarter of the space to grow. Palm oil could meet the world's demand for vegetable oil with just one-fourth of the land we currently use for other vegetable oil crops like soy, corn, olive, and sunflower.

If we got all our vegetable oil from soybeans, we would need almost 60 percent more vegetable oil land than we use now. By growing palm oil instead of other types of oil crops, we can use less land to grow more vegetable oil. If we want to use the least land to grow the most vegetable oil, it makes the most sense to get it from palm oil. But palm oil trees can only grow in

Palm oil plantation in Malaysia.

a few places because of the rainy climate they need. These are places like Indonesia, where orangutans live.

Growing palm oil trees also produces jobs for Indonesian farmers and loggers. As in Brazil, the people who deforest Indonesia are often poor and have very few other ways to earn money. Stopping deforestation is great for the forests, but it puts people out of work.

But there are ways to provide those jobs without new deforestation. Malaysia, a country near Indonesia, is also a major producer of palm oil, but it has strong restrictions on deforestation, and most of its palm oil is not grown on recently deforested land. By producing palm oil more sustainably, Malaysia protects its forests while supplying new jobs.

Forests can provide jobs, too. Ecotourism is a growing industry that uses forests while keeping them intact by helping people visit places to see nature. Travelers pay local people to guide them through the forests, tell them about the animals living there, and cook local foods.

There are no easy solutions to these problems, and they are all a part of climate change. It takes people from many countries, working together, to solve these issues. The sooner we start trying to solve them, the sooner we will be able to find answers and start making changes. We can all help.

WANGARI MAATHAI

Some places around the world are actively practicing reforestation, the planting of new trees to replace lost ones. One of the most well-known champions of reforestation was Dr. Wangari Maathai. Born in Kenya in 1940, she founded the Green Belt Movement and was the first African woman to win the Nobel Peace Prize. The Green Belt Movement helps women in rural Kenya plant trees and teaches about the sustainable use of natural resources.

Dr. Maathai founded the movement after learning that the women of rural Kenya had to travel farther for firewood each year and that their streams were drying up. The movement is responsible for planting millions of trees in Kenya and paying local people to plant millions more. Her legacy is still felt in Kenya and many communities across Africa that benefit from reforestation.

Nobel Laureate Dr. Wangari Maathai

CALL TO ACTION!

REDUCE DEFORESTATION

People can reduce the impact of deforestation through the food they eat, the clothes they wear, and what they buy. Sometimes, the decision not to buy anything at all can be the most powerful decision you can make. If many people decide not to buy something or buy only sustainable products made without deforestation, this becomes powerful. It is called voting with your wallet. Encouraging people to be mindful of products they buy can be a great way to reduce deforestation.

CALL TO ACTION!

PRACTICE REFORESTATION

Trees are one of the most effective natural tools we have to fight climate change because trees take in carbon dioxide and pollutants like smog and give out clean air. Plants also need carbon dioxide to make their own food, so they act like vacuums for greenhouse gases. Trees can also live for hundreds of years, providing habitats for animals, filtering water, and protecting soil. Some trees also provide fruit and nuts for people and animals to eat.

If forests are at risk, people can campaign to protect these lands by writing letters to government officials and going to local meetings. People can fundraise money to buy land to save trees. Saving existing wilderness is a great way to prevent future deforestation.

You can organize Adopt-A-Tree Clubs. There may be empty spaces in your community, like abandoned farms or houses, or parking lots. Your group can write to local governments, organize community meetings, and work with your local park district to turn these vacant spaces into natural areas by replanting native trees or making a sustainable community. Your school can plant new trees on its own property, local park districts can plant new trees, and private citizens can plant trees on their land.

CHAPTER 9

TRANSPORTATION PiLEUP

Another way to help fight climate change is for people to switch their kind of transportation, because the transportation sector produces about 15 percent of the world's greenhouse gas emissions.

About 30 percent of the world's energy comes from oil. 23 percent comes from natural gas, and 26 percent comes from coal; the rest comes from renewables and nuclear power. One of the biggest users of oil around the world is the transportation sector, or vehicles being used to move people, products, and resources. Gasoline, diesel fuel, and natural gas are the most common fossil fuels used in transportation.

All the trucks, cars, buses, planes, trains, and ships around the world produce over seven billion tons of carbon dioxide and other greenhouse gases every year. Almost every method of transportation is powered by burning fossil fuels. Roughly 7 percent of all greenhouse gas emissions come from personal cars—the largest part of the transportation sector's contribution to climate change. Minivans and pickup trucks used for business are a small part of the much bigger problem.

Scientists estimate that there are about one-and-one half billion personal cars on the road globally. Reducing emissions from personal vehicles is the most efficient option to reduce transportation emissions. But some people may drive cars because they do not have any other choice in how they get to where they need to go.

The COVID-19 pandemic showed that reducing road traffic during lockdowns reduced pollution from transportation. In 2020, the world saw a 7 percent reduction in carbon dioxide emissions, most of which can

be attributed to a reduction in the use of cars and tranportation. However, this drop was only temporary, and in 2021 more carbon dioxide was emitted annually than before the pandemic.

There is no easy way to reduce the greenhouse gases from personal vehicles, but there are possibilities to explore, like reducing driving or switching to electric vehicles.

ELECTRIC VEHICLES AND ALTERNATIVE FUELS

Renewable energy sources like wind turbines and solar panels are environmentally friendly alternatives that produce constant electricity for buildings. And there are sustainable alternatives for transportation.

Instead of using cars that require liquid fuel, as we have been, we could use electric vehicles. Electricity is stored in batteries that can be recharged at any power grid. This is happening globally.

Scientists are working on powering planes with hydrogen, a liquid fuel that can be made without fossil fuels, though it is very difficult to use.

The next biggest component of the transportation sector is made up of the semitrucks that haul goods to the grocery store or deliver furniture. These trucks are used around the world. Without trucks, people in cities would be unable to get food from farms. But these trucks also produce 5 percent of the world's total greenhouse gas emissions.

This creates an interesting problem with transportation,

called the "last mile" problem. As vehicles become larger, from cars to trucks to trains to enormous container ships, they can carry more goods farther distances while using less fuel. Shipping vessels are one of the most efficient forms of transportation, hauling millions of tons of goods every year and producing only 2 percent of all greenhouse gas emissions. Trains are also very efficient, producing a little less than 0.5 percent of total greenhouse gases.

MEXICO

Following one avocado as it ships from a farm in Mexico to a grocery store in Paris, France, the most greenhouse gas emissions on this journey are used by the truck that takes the avocado from the nearby port into the city. Most of the greenhouse gas emissions are in the "last mile" of shipping, which is handled by trucks.

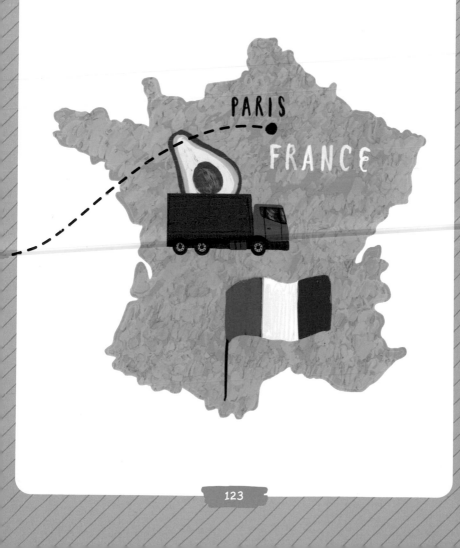

This "last mile" problem is why trucks produce 5 percent of the world's greenhouse gases. People live far apart in many different places and need many different trucks to haul all kinds of products, using more fuel. Running these trucks on electricity is the best option to reduce emissions. But it is still too expensive for most companies to use electric trucks.

CHAPTER 10

AiR POLLUTION

Air pollution affects climate change by changing our cloud cover, changing what our atmosphere and oceans are made of, and damaging the way our trees absorb carbon dioxide.

When factories, cars, trains, planes, and power plants burn fossil fuels, they also produce other kinds of gases that enter the atmosphere, all called air pollution. Air pollution has a direct negative effect on human health.

Air pollution can be tiny particles of matter that get caught in our throats and lungs, like smoke, or it can be chemicals that damage our cells. It contributes to climate change, causes smog, and can make people sick.

While greenhouse gases are technically a kind of air pollution, scientists consider greenhouse gases to be different than what we think of as air pollution. This is because, even though greenhouse gases enter the atmosphere and worsen climate change, it is safe to breathe in normal amounts of most greenhouse gases, like carbon dioxide or methane. These gases are only harmful to humans at huge volumes in small spaces. It is very unusual to see dangerous volumes of greenhouse gases in everyday life. They do not cause cancer or block out the sky, like air pollution does,

Air pollutants like the chemicals from gasoline or the particles in smoke cause more immediate problems. These problems can range from city smog to birth defects in babies. These kinds of air pollution are dangerous even in small amounts.

So even though they come from the same source—burning fossil fuels—greenhouse gas emissions are separate from air pollution. Air pollution is a side effect of burning fossil fuels. Greenhouse gas emissions from burning fossil fuels cause climate change, but air pollution, also from burning those same fossil fuels, is tied to wider human impacts of climate change. If we want to stop air pollution, we also need

ACID RAIN

....

The fight against acid rain is a good example of new laws helping the earth. In the 1970s, the United States enacted laws that limited how much damaging chemicals our factories and power plants could produce. These chemicals caused acid rain, which kills plants and animals. Soon after these laws were passed, acid rain in the United States ended.

to stop greenhouse gas emissions.

Air pollution can hurt people and the environment around us, and it is deeply connected to climate change. If we want to protect as many people and animals as possible, we need to stop both climate change and air pollution. Since they are so connected, this is one of the few times when we can address two problems with one solution.

Of course, most problems are not this straightforward.

The Effects of Air Pollution

Imagine you live in the Indian state of Punjab, in the city of Jalandhar. You have spent your entire life in the city, living among the hundreds of thousands of people there. Every day, you walk to school, and you can taste the smoke and dust from cars, factories, and farms that burn the leftovers from harvest

However, not all countries have these laws, so acid rain is still a problem in places with a lot of air pollution, like China or Russia. Acid rain is an example of how air pollution can also make climate change worse. Not only can air pollution kill people, but it can kill forests that suck up carbon dioxide, making it harder to fight climate change.

in the air. A layer of smog hangs over the city.

You know that the Himalayas, the tallest mountain range on Earth, are just one hundred miles from Jalandhar. Adults and teachers at school talk about how, many years ago, people could see the mountain range from the city. You have never seen it. The smog from the city is so thick that the horizon is hazy. On really bad days, the sky is a dirty yellow.

In 2020, the global pandemic caused by the COVID-19 virus forced the Indian government, along with much of the rest of the world, to shut down nonessential travel and businesses across the country to try to stop the spread of the virus. As a result, there were fewer cars on the road and factories temporarily shut.

One day in 2020, you walk to a hill near your house, look north, and you can see them for the first time: the Himalayas, the most extreme and famous mountains on Earth. For the first time in decades, everyone in the city can see the mountains from their own homes because the smog has cleared enough.

Months later, as the lockdowns ease and people return to their cars and jobs, the smog over the city returns. The Himalayas are no longer visible.

But air pollution is more than smog, and it causes bigger problems than not being able to see mountains. Air pollution can cause cancer, make breathing difficult, and even turn into greenhouse gases over time.

Most air pollution comes from vehicles like trucks and cars that burn gasoline, which, besides producing greenhouse gases, also produce chemicals including carbon monoxide. Lots of cars in one place, such as in a city, can create major problems like lung-damaging smog. Burning fossil fuels in power plants releases these same chemicals. Coal is often especially high in chemicals that can be emitted as air pollution when coal is burned. Air pollution creates other health problems, like brain damage, nerve damage, and birth defects.

Another source of air pollution is smoke from wood-burning fires. Wood smoke can come from wildfires, some factories and power plants, or fires in homes used for cooking or heating. Even breathing in a little smoke over a long time can cause lung diseases. Tiny particles in wood smoke can

also block out light, giving smog its dark appearance.

Accidental wildfires around the world also produce air pollution and greenhouse gases. In 2020, wildfires in California released more than 100,000,000 tons of greenhouse gases and put west coast cities on lockdown due to unsafe levels of air pollution. Natural wildfires can be helpful to the environment, removing dead plant matter and freeing up nutrients. However, governments including the United States have banned natural fires for years. Without these natural fires, ultra-hot wildfires, so hot that they can cause trees to explode, are springing up around the world. And as climate change makes the world hotter and drier, wildfires are only going to get worse.

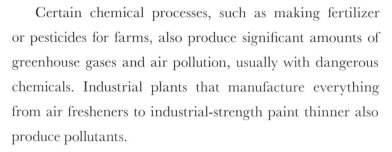

Certain chemical processes, such as making fertilizer or pesticides for farms, also produce significant amounts of greenhouse gases and air pollution, usually with dangerous chemicals. Industrial plants that manufacture everything from air fresheners to industrial-strength paint thinner also produce pollutants.

These pollutants interact with other chemicals in air pollution to produce ground-level ozone, the ingredient of smog that blocks out the sun and does major damage to people's lungs if they breathe in a lot of it. Ozone high in the atmosphere is helpful because it blocks ultraviolet radiation, but it too would cause lung damage if you breathed it. Ozone does not naturally occur at ground level, meaning that ground-level ozone is made by people.

The many kinds of air pollution come from different sources, but they all tend to have the same effect: they make people sick when they are breathed. The World Health Organization (WHO) says that millions of people die every year from problems related to air pollution and that this

WESTERN NORTH AMERICA'S TRIBES

In the United States, native peoples have practiced religious and cultural fire ceremonies for thousands of years. The Mono Indians of California, along with other California tribes like the Yurok, midwestern groups like the Potawatomi Nation, and southwestern groups like the Jemez Pueblo, all know that fire is important to keep land healthy. They knew long before scientists did that fires are crucial to some healthy ecosystems.

Not every ecosystem needs fire to survive. Wetter ecosystems, like rain forests, can be damaged by fire. But most other ecosystems, from pine forests to prairies, need fire to thrive.

These native peoples were stewards of the land before European colonizers arrived, and since then the American government has banned their fire customs for many years. The land needs fire; taking it away results in much bigger fires in the future.

In more recent years, the American government has been working with native groups to practice their fire customs and controlled burns. This allows indigenous peoples to practice their own cultures and to prevent massive wildfires. Supporting local controlled fires and practicing fire safety is one way that people can help indigenous communities fight climate change.

A firefighter drops flame from a driptorch in a forested area

number will probably get higher as poorer countries start to burn more fossil fuels. Not only does burning fossil fuels make climate change worse, but it is also hurting people.

Cleaner ways of burning fossil fuels are great temporary solutions but ultimately are not enough. Power plants around the world are still polluting even though cleaner energy is available. We need to use fuel sources that are sustainable and do not produce air pollution, like wind or solar energy. But in the short term, we can find ways to use less fossil fuels and use them more cleanly when we can.

CALL TO ACTION!

A BIKE, A BUS, A TRAIN

Not everyone needs a car. Some people can walk or bike to work or school. But if someone needs to travel a little bit farther, taking a bus or train instead of driving is a great way to reduce carbon emissions.

Cities with strong public transportation systems reduce their smog because there are fewer cars on the road. If people can travel by affordable bus or train, personal cars are less necessary, and the emissions from personal cars can be reduced. Starting a club to get cities to develop new, sustainable, affordable forms of public transportation like electric buses and trams, and getting more people to use public transportation are ways to reduce air pollution from transportation.

POWER (anD ThE PROBLEM)

For much of the world, factories make everything we use in our daily lives, from computers to clothes. Industries, or businesses that make things or their ingredients, use immense amounts of electricity generated by fossil fuels and power plants—they produce as much as 24 percent of greenhouse gas emissions worldwide and, in some countries, consume as much as 35 percent of all electricity. Making electricity is the single largest creator of greenhouse gases worldwide.

The amount of information about these factories and the products they produce is now more available than it once was. If people know the impacts of their purchases on our environment, they can pressure businesses to be more sustainable.

Since industry is a leading cause of climate change, understanding how best to fight climate change includes understanding how and why industry produces so much greenhouse gas.

Energy in Industry

Anything that uses fossil fuel electricity produces greenhouse gases.

Some factories, such as cement or steel manufacturers, burn fossil fuels directly, but many factories get their energy from power plants. Power plants are places that burn fossil fuels to produce electricity and then distribute it through wires, power stations, and electrical transformers across hundreds or thousands of miles. This allows electricity to be used almost everywhere, but it also poses a major problem.

As much as 5 percent of the electricity generated by a power plant can be "lost" between the power plant and the homes and businesses to which it supplies power, and as much as 50 percent of the energy from burning fossil fuels is not even turned into electricity. This is due mostly to heat loss.

Burning coal produces electricity by heating water to turn the water into steam. The steam rises, pushing on massive electrical generators that spin and create electricity to power homes and businesses.

Not all the heat from the burning coal goes directly to the water. Heat naturally flows into everything around it, and heat cannot be perfectly contained. Some of this lost heat leaves the water and steam and goes into the factory pipes, the air of the factory, and the generator itself.

This is one of the reasons why creating electricity produces so much greenhouse gas. For any amount of fossil fuels burned, as much as half that energy is lost. So more must be burned and it is turned into greenhouse gases. Of all the electricity used by industry, anywhere from 5 to 25 percent is used just to mine and process more fossil fuels to make more electricity.

Besides losing some energy to heat and having to make more electricity by burning more fossil fuels, factories use a lot

of electricity to run their machinery. This produces most of their greenhouse gases. In the United States, 77 percent of the electricity used by industry is used during the making of products. The rest is used for mining and construction, and a small percentage is used for agriculture.

Of that 77 percent of electricity used in manufacturing, 37 percent is used to make chemicals like paints, glues, or cleaning supplies. The rest is used to manufacture fossil fuels, paper, metals, cements, and household products. Building anything from simple things like mattresses to complex items like cell phones produces a lot of greenhouse gas.

Energy production is the biggest producer of global greenhouse gases. Industry is responsible for 24 percent of all greenhouse gas emissions. Industry produces greenhouse gases in many different ways. People have control over this by not buying products that produce a lot of greenhouse gases and by voting for candidates who support greenhouse gas emissions regulations. And people have control over their own homes.

Energy at Home

Homes produce 11 percent of greenhouse gases. Because we burn fossil fuels to produce electricity, greenhouse gases come from anything using electricity. Most of this electricity is used in heating and cooling.

Another chunk of energy used in homes comes from heating water. Air conditioners and refrigerators also use immense amounts of electricity, in addition to releasing fluorinated gases, or very strong greenhouse gases.

Lighting homes also uses energy. Powering electronic devices such as microwaves, computers, cell phones, vacuums, and televisions uses even more.

Most energy in the average commercial building goes to maintaining the building's temperature and keeping lights on.

Some buildings use the most energy powering electronics, such as computers.

The best way to stop climate change and make the biggest difference is to reduce electricity made by burning fossil fuels. If we could stop burning fossil fuels, almost all the greenhouse gases produced by industry and buildings—around 50 percent of all greenhouse gas emissions—would stop being a problem.

Using less energy in your home, buying fewer new products and choosing reusable or recycled ones, or switching to

renewable energy options are great ways to reduce your own environmental impact. But we can do even more when we work together.

Stopping the use of fossil fuels would change the world for the better, but it would have its own problems, like the time and money it would take to build renewable energy sources. Even if we stopped burning fossil fuels immediately, it would not solve every problem, like garbage and water pollution.

CALL TO ACTION!

TURN OFF THOSE LIGHTS

Because energy use is the biggest cause of climate change, using less energy is one of the best ways to make a big impact.

Explain to people that they can use less energy in their homes by turning off lights, buying electronics that use less electricity, using heaters and air conditioners less, purchasing renewable energy, and using less hot water.

CHAPTER 12

WATER AT THE BOTTOM OF THE OCEAN

The deepest known part of the world's oceans is the Challenger Deep, over 35,000 feet below the surface. Very few people have been there. It is one of the most extreme places on Earth and is still full of life. But the Challenger Deep also has plastic bags.

In 2019, scientists visiting the Challenger Deep discovered plastic grocery store bags at the bottom of the ocean, one

of the spots farthest away from people. The bags were there because our planet is covered in plastics, from the bottom of the ocean to the top of Mount Everest, to the insides of turtles' bodies and around the heads of dolphins, to the fish that we eat at dinner—plastics from humans are everywhere. They are killing both animals and ecosystems.

All the water on Earth is connected by the water cycle, moving water all over the planet. We have the same water now that the earth has had for billions of years because of the water cycle.

Most of the water on Earth stays in the oceans. About 70 percent of the planet is covered by water, and 97 percent of all water on Earth is in the oceans. Because an ocean is salty, this is salt water, water we cannot drink or use for agriculture or industry.

Less than 1 percent of water is drinkable.

Water evaporates from the ocean into the atmosphere, where it becomes water vapor. Water vapor can stay in the atmosphere and travel around the earth, but eventually it falls out of the atmosphere as precipitation, either as fog, rain, snow, or mixtures like sleet. If snow lands and doesn't melt, or if water freezes, it can form glaciers at the north or south poles. This frozen water never used to melt. However, as climate change warms our planet, this ice turns back into water, causing sea levels to rise.

There is more than enough fresh water on Earth for everyone to drink, but it's not evenly distributed. Countries like Saudi Arabia and places like California have dry climates and tend not to have enough water for everyone. A lot of water is also used in agriculture and industry. But water is threatened by climate change.

Civilization relies on regular levels of fresh water. People need water from rain, rivers, and lakes, or groundwater to survive, but many places are using up their water sources. Water is being overused by agriculture and industry. The Aral Sea near Kazakhstan has disappeared because people took the water from its rivers. The Punjab region in India is seeing its farms fail because people have been using too much water from aquifers.

Indonesia is changing its capital city, Jakarta, to Nusantara, because Jakarta is sinking due to so much groundwater being removed from underground by agriculture. Jakarta is a coastal city, so as it sinks it is even more at risk from the rise of the sea level. This creates many new problems, including moving millions of people.

The biggest threat to fresh water is from climate change. As the planet warms up and more water evaporates, droughts are becoming more common. Heat waves and less rainfall are becoming more extreme, leading to less surface water and also less groundwater. Water sources such as lakes and rivers are drying up, and places that once relied on yearly rains can no longer plan on that rain. The most extreme example of this is Cape Town's Day Zero drought disaster.

Cape Town, a major city in South Africa, relies on winter rains to refill its water reservoirs for its millions of people. However, as more people moved to the city and industry and agriculture used more water, the reservoirs struggled to meet demand. Then, a series of extreme droughts in 2015, 2016, and 2017 left the reservoirs at critically low levels.

Cape Town was forced to cut the amount of water it used by 50 percent. By 2018, the city was weeks away from running out of water. If Cape Town had reached "Day Zero," it would have shut off city water, forcing people to travel for their water.

Thankfully, with reduced water usage and rains, Cape Town avoided Day Zero. Reducing water was not an easy solution; people struggled with severe limits and food production was reduced to save water.

Climate change is making droughts more common everywhere. More cities are having to reduce water usage. We have to prepare for climate change so we don't run out of water.

Droughts may be the biggest threat from climate change, yet they are just one reason why we have to start changing our lifestyles now. But there are other threats to the world's water.

Plastics Are Forever

Oceans face other threats. Because all water leads to the oceans, any pollution on land eventually reaches the oceans. Two obvious threats are industrial liquid wastes and solid plastic pollution.

Industry produces immense amounts of liquid pollution, from chemicals to manure from cattle. Only some of the pollution is made up of plastics. Part of it is made up of chemicals from industrial waste that is poured directly into the water, most of it untreated, or that still has chemicals from industry in it.

Debris and garbage wash up along the banks of the Mississippi River.

WINONA LADUKE

Born in 1959, Winona LaDuke is an environmental activist and member of the White Earth Reservation, an indigenous Ojibwe group in Minnesota. She has spent her life promoting indigenous rights and fighting for the environment. Together with her organization Honor the Earth, she has worked to restore original Ojibwe land to its natural state, provide sustainable energy for her people, and promote the growth of wild rice, a staple of Ojibwe cultures that has been threatened by leakage from pipelines mixing with the water used to grow the rice.

LaDuke opposes the expansion of fossil fuel projects. She has fought the construction of oil pipelines across the United States, developing a network of people called Water Protectors to help protect fresh water in the United States from oil pollution.

Winona LaDuke, cofounder of Honor the Earth. Germany, 1970s.

Mines, chemical processing plants, and oil pipelines constantly leak dangerous chemicals and fossil fuels into surface water and groundwater, making this water undrinkable. Major rivers in Asia, like the Ganges and the Yangtze, are threatened by waste from factories and farms and even the Mississippi River is polluted by oil pipelines and chemical plants. Among the biggest sources of industrial waste are farms. When it rains on land, fertilizers and pesticides that can kill plants and animals get sucked into rivers and streams, which eventually lead to the ocean.

Ocean pollution is made worse by the burning of fossil fuels that cause climate change, and it is also making climate change worse.

Runoff, or water from rain and irrigation that travels along the ground, collects chemicals such as the fertilizers used in agriculture and can cause algae to grow in huge numbers. These algae eventually die and, as they decompose, they use all the oxygen in the water. This kills millions of fish and other sea creatures every year. But this pollution is not limited to fish; when people eat fish affected by pollution, people consume some of that pollution. The chemicals from pesticides and factory waste can cause cancer, developmental and neurological damage, and even infertility. This movement of pollutants up the food chain is called biomagnification.

Solid plastic pollution is a big industrial problem facing

the earth. It is related to climate change because fossil fuels are used to make plastics, contributing to global warming. But plastics also damage the earth and make climate change worse in other ways.

Solid garbage of all kinds ends up in the oceans and other bodies of water, but plastic is the worst solid waste. In addition to fossil fuels, chemicals are also used to make plastics. When the plastics decompose, or break down, they release these chemicals. Plastics and their chemicals can take from between twenty to six hundred years to fully decompose. Internationally banned chemicals are still in our oceans, along with the plastic.

There are many single-use plastic items, like plastic water bottles, bags, and utensils, in our oceans, all made to be used once and thrown away. Cigarette butts are another major form of plastic waste that ends up in the oceans, along with fishing line. Most of the plastic comes from people littering and factories' waste. It is pulled to the oceans by the water cycle.

Scientists think that about 9 to 13 tons of plastic enter the oceans every year. As much as 90 percent may be from single-use plastics that are eaten by sea animals like turtles. The animals mistake the plastic items for food and often choke to death.

These plastics sometimes stay in one piece, or they break down into tiny microplastics.

Plastic in the oceans is difficult to clean up because the oceans are so vast, but microplastics are especially difficult to clean up. The Great Pacific Garbage Patch in the central Pacific, where ocean currents push plastics together, is twice the size of Texas, and it is mostly microplastics. Scientists think there may be more than twenty-five trillion pieces of microplastics in the oceans worldwide.

Microplastics cause an even worse problem than larger

CALL TO ACTION!

GARBAGE

Because almost all pollution that ends up in the water cycle eventually reaches the oceans, one way to help stop water pollution is to reduce the amount of garbage. If you already are part of a club, encourage people to be aware of where their trash goes, to use less things that need to be thrown out and that cannot be recycled, and to convince local governments and businesses to produce less waste.

Writing to local governments to stop new fossil fuel developments that pollute water, like oil pipelines or coal mines, helps stop pollution. Encourage your school to do waste counts where garbage is weighed and containers are counted—present this to people to convince them to reduce and recycle waste. Your club can advocate for no-dumping laws, which stop people and companies from dumping dangerous chemicals down drains and into water supplies.

CIRCULAR ECONOMIES

One way to reduce waste is for businesses to invest in creating circular economies, where the waste from one part of the system becomes the ingredients for another part of the system. For example, people are starting businesses around the world that take plastic waste and turn it into bricks, which can be used to build roads and houses. By turning waste into something useful, we reduce pollution and garbage.

Installing circular economies is not very common. They are difficult to install because they require a lot of work. It is easier to throw out something than to develop systems to collect waste, transport it to a new business site, separate it, turn it into a different product, and then find a way to dispose of that new product.

MAKE YOUR OWN BIRDFEEDER

ADD STRING

ADD FEED

1 WASH OUT AN OLD MILK JUG

2 USE SCISSORS TO CUT A LARGE HOLE

3 PUT MASKING TAPE AROUND SHARP EDGES

pieces of plastic because every ocean animal eats them. Microplastics can cause neurological issues, developmental damage, cancer, and infertility in animals. But they can also be biomagnified. Shrimp eat microplastics, bigger fish eat the shrimp, and we eat those fish. This means we eat the microplastics too. The average person consumes thousands of microplastics every year. When scientists studied a sample of human bodies, they found microplastics in every part of the bodies. Plastics are inside us.

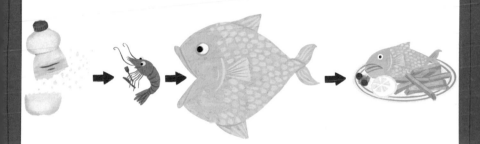

Despite how much plastic ends up in the oceans, it is only a small percentage of the total plastic produced. Humans create more than three hundred seventy-five million tons of plastic every year. Most of it is thrown out. In the United States, only 9 percent of plastic is recycled. The rest goes into landfills, where it will sit for hundreds of years before it decomposes, leaking chemicals the whole time. Most of the plastics in the oceans come from low-income countries, like India or the Philippines, where there are many people but no infrastructure to take plastics to landfills. In some places, plastics are burned for energy, which releases greenhouse gases and other harmful chemicals into the air, but most end up in landfills or oceans.

Solutions are difficult. Civilization relies on plastics. Food comes in plastic containers, computers and cars use plastic pieces, and some clothes are made of plastics. We can't stop making plastics entirely, but finding non-fossil fuel and bio-degradable plastics or else recycling more plastics are ways to keep them out of oceans and out of us and other animals. There are biodegradable plastics, but they can still take dozens of years to decompose and can still damage oceans. Recycling plastics is difficult, expensive, and only effective some of the time. The best way to reduce our plastic pollution is to use fewer plastics.

Protecting our oceans is one of the best things we can do to fight climate change. The oceans are one of the single greatest tools our planet has to control greenhouse gases.

Plastics for Breakfast

Ocean ecosystems provide many benefits. They give millions of people who live on coasts food to eat and

jobs to do, they move nutrients around the planet, and they suck up carbon dioxide from the atmosphere.

Carbon dioxide enters the oceans on its own and dissolves naturally in water. Cold water absorbs more carbon dioxide than warm water. Ocean currents that move water across the planet also move carbon dioxide to the bottom of the oceans. It can stay there, out of the atmosphere for thousands of years, or even longer if it becomes part of the ocean floor by reacting with ocean sediment.

Algae and phytoplankton, or tiny organisms that make their own food, also suck up carbon dioxide. When these creatures die, they are eaten by other creatures or sink to the bottom of the oceans, which in turn keeps carbon dioxide out of the atmosphere.

With these processes, oceans can remove billions of tons of carbon dioxide, slowing climate change.

But we are destroying the natural tools we have to fight climate change through oceans. Because the ocean is warming and colder water is better at sucking up carbon dioxide, climate change makes it more difficult for the warming ocean to absorb greenhouse gases. Climate change is slowing down ocean currents, also making it more difficult to store that carbon at the bottom of the ocean. It is also disrupting ocean ecosystems like coral reefs and kelp forests, which rely on these currents to bring them food. Without food, these ecosystems that suck up carbon dioxide and provide homes for animals cannot survive. Kelp forests and algal zones, places where algae naturally grow in large quantities, are some of the most powerful greenhouse gas sinks on Earth, taking out more carbon dioxide than forests. But they require a vast network of ecosystems, species, and currents to work properly.

We are also killing ocean ecosystems in other ways. Plastic pollution and chemical pollution from farms and factories threaten ocean life. Over-fishing and using nets that scrape along the bottom of the ocean to catch fish, called bottom trawling, also trap dolphins and seals.

Because the earth is so connected, no ecosystems are truly separate from each other. A coral reef relies on ocean currents to bring nutrients. That coral reef provides homes for fish and breeding grounds for sea creatures like turtles and sharks, which move to open oceans and help to keep algal zones healthy. Damaging one part of the earth affects many other parts.

95 percent of California's kelp forests have disappeared. They once absorbed huge amounts of carbon dioxide from the atmosphere.

The biggest threat to kelp forests are purple urchins, which eat kelp. Normally, sea stars eat purple urchins. But because of warming oceans, there are less sea stars to eat the purple urchins, who are left to destroy the kelp forests that fight climate change.

Other species killed by ocean pollution are also interconnected. Ocean animals get stuck in plastic bags, sea birds get their heads caught in plastic bottles, whales drown in fishing nets, sea turtles eat plastic bags, and otters that eat purple urchins get tangled in fishing line. The ocean needs these animals to keep ecosystems alive and to absorb carbon dioxide.

The Last of the Corals

Coral reefs are crucial parts of ocean ecosystems, providing homes for millions of animals, and helping suck up carbon dioxide. Their biggest threat is carbon dioxide.

Corals are very sensitive to environmental changes. As the warming oceans absorb more of the carbon dioxide that we are adding to the atmosphere, the oceans become slightly more acidic. Climate change and ocean acidification are killing coral reefs.

The environment is changing too quickly for corals to adapt. Scientists predict that as many as 99 percent of corals will be extinct by 2050. The only corals that may survive are deep-water corals—the oceans will never be the same without

coral reefs and all the animals who make the reefs their home.

The risk of losing species forever goes beyond corals. Everything in our world is connected. Human destruction of our planet has driven thousands of species of plants and animals to extinction, killing every animal in that species, including some species we have never seen. Climate change and habitat destruction due to pollution and deforestation are the leading causes of the extinction of animals.

Because we do not know how exactly many animal species there are, we do not know how many are extinct or soon will be. Scientists estimate at least five hundred species have become extinct since 1750, but we could be losing as many as one thousand species every year. Normally, fewer than

ten animals should become extinct every year due to natural causes. Animals at risk of dying out are called endangered. Hundreds of species of endangered animals, from elephants and whales to parrots and frogs, could all become extinct in the next fifty years.

Scientists predict that future extinctions of animals may be even greater. Some new scientific studies predict that if greenhouse gas emissions continue to increase at the same rate they are now, global warming could cause the largest extinction of ocean animals since about 250 million years ago, when about 90 percent of ocean life died in oceans that were too hot, too acidic, and lacking in oxygen. That was the worst mass extinction in Earth's history, killing more than 50 percent of all animals, including 70 percent of land vertebrates, or animals with backbones.

Rendering of the Dodo Bird circa 1917.

ABORIGINAL AUSTRALIANS AND TORRES STRAIT ISLANDERS

The loss of Australia's Great Barrier Reef, which scientists predict may die by 2050, would be the loss of a major cultural center for the Torres Strait Islander and Aboriginal Australian peoples, who have lived on Australia, Papua New Guinea, and nearby islands for thousands of years. The Great Barrier Reef is central to their culture and life.

These indigenous peoples lived here before the reef existed, leaving artifacts that are now buried beneath the reef. Since the reef formed, the people have lived off its resources. It has become part of their culture and spirituality. These native peoples are fighting climate change to protect nature and their cultures.

A lithograph of Aboriginal Australians of Port Phillip, Victoria.

This change could have happened because of volcanoes erupting for millions of years, sending carbon dioxide into the atmosphere. But the carbon dioxide we are putting into the atmosphere now is about two times as much as it was then.

The temperatures and oxygen levels in our oceans are already dangerously high for coral life and other ocean species.

Scientists believe that humans are causing a sixth mass extinction through our unsustainable use of land, water, and energy and through climate change. This would affect not just our oceans, but land animals, too.

We are already seeing the effects of a sixth mass extinction today. In 2021, the United States' Pacific Northwest region, as well as British Columbia in Canada, experienced a record-breaking heat wave from late June until the middle of July with temperatures reaching over 110 degrees Fahrenheit. This was a heat wave that happens only once every 1,000 years, and it was made worse by climate change. The heat caused wildfires; killed more than 1,400 people; destroyed towns, roads, and railroads; burned crops; and closed businesses, and biologists estimate that this heat wave killed as many as one billion ocean creatures. Many of these creatures were small, like barnacles or mussels, causing the larger animals that eat the small ones to die from lack of food. Catastrophes like this happen around the world.

But we can stop this sixth mass extinction by starting to act now. If we significantly reduce the burning of fossil fuels and the amount of carbon dioxide we release into the atmosphere, scientists predict we can lessen the chance of this mass extinction by as much as 70 percent. We need to stop Earth from warming even more than it already has, and everyone can play a part in that.

Our world needs plants and animals to survive and to fight climate change. Healthy ecosystems rely on biodiversity, or having many different species, to stay balanced and fight diseases and natural disasters These healthy ecosystems then fight climate change by absorbing carbon dioxide through plants like trees and grasses. Fighting pollution is one way to help the oceans, but protecting animals and their habitats around the world is a crucial step in the process too. Ecosystems need plants and animals to spread seeds, remove sick or dying plants, and prevent any single kind of plant from taking over.

CALL TO ACTION!

STOPPING EXTINCTION

Cleaning up garbage on the beach is a helpful short-term solution, but we need to do more to keep garbage off the beach permanently.

One option is to allocate funds for legal protection of wild areas in county, state, or national parks. You can form a group in your school or community to get governments to restore and protect natural land and allocate funds for its long-term protection so endangered animals have safe places to live.

But places without garbage also need help. Your club or group can work to restore local natural habitats by appealing to governments and businesses to help keep them clean. Replanting kelp forests in the ocean is one good way to fight climate change and protect local habitats.

CHAPTER 13

THE FUTURE OF OUR PLANET

Looking at Earth from space, our planet is a little blue dot. For more than one hundred thousand years, humans have lived on Earth, overcoming many challenges. Climate change is a big challenge.

There are many problems. The great rain forests are being cut down. Animals are dying, and our pollution is infecting the water and making the air we breathe toxic. Industry,

agriculture, and transportation cause problems. Droughts are longer and hotter; storms, more powerful. The sea levels rise, threatening to swallow many places around the globe. People have to leave their homes because of these weather events. The climate is less stable.

The scale of climate change is huge. Our need for fossil fuels that drives so much of climate change causes immense problems.

But there are solutions to these problems, even though they are not easy. The most effective measure would be to stop burning fossil fuels so we stop producing new greenhouse gases and to start building renewable energy technologies instead so that cities could run on renewable energy. Governments would need to help people learn new jobs to replace their old ones, and help poorer people. We would need to build huge solar fields to produce electricity without fossil fuels. Governments could provide people with wind turbines. Plants could cover the walls of skyscrapers. Once fossil fuels were no long emitting greenhouse gases, we could start taking existing greenhouse gases out of the atmosphere by planting new forests where farmland used to be and growing kelp forests along the coasts. We could grow vegetables in community farms, plant trees across mountainsides, and rebuild coral reefs. All these actions would give people jobs.

But these solutions are expensive, long-term, and would

THE MAASAI OF AFRICA

Africa has hundreds of different native groups and cultures, all of whom are affected by climate change. The Maasai are already affected. They live in the plains of Kenya and Tanzania where they practice their traditional lifestyle of herding African cattle through expansive grasslands. They live almost entirely off these cattle.

However, as climate change causes rains to become scarce and droughts to become longer, the grasslands are drying up, and the Maasai cattle are dying. It is more difficult to live the traditional Maasai lifestyle. But the Maasai are fighting back against climate change by protecting their land and preparing for drought by developing relief funds to replace cattle lost to droughts and by conserving more land where they can protect larger ecosystems.

A Maasai herdsman.

require governments to work together. It is therefore doubtful that these actions will be taken.

This makes it important for each of us to do everything we can to safeguard our world, making it sustainable. People working together is the most powerful force on Earth.

Adaptation and Resiliency

Because consequences of climate change have already started, our best tools against them are adaptation and resiliency.

Planning to live with climate change is planning to adapt. We can get used to living in a new climate: cities moving inland to avoid sea level rise, island countries building upward to escape rising waters, coastal cities investing in flood control measures, and inland cities storing rainwater and growing new forests. Right now, Ethiopia, Nigeria, and Sudan are trying to grow a forest across the African continent to stop the Sahara desert from expanding.

Adaptation goes along with resilience, or being able to bounce back. Countries have to be resilient to disasters. If disaster strikes, it isn't enough to just be prepared—we must build back stronger than before.

In 2021, Texas had a terrible winter storm. Millions of people lost their power sources, and it took weeks to repair them. People froze to death and choked on fumes from fires they built in their homes, trying to keep warm. The electricity

infrastructure failed when faced with severe weather. Because severe weather increases with climate change, we need systems suited to face threats.

Texas has not built back stronger. It is unlikely the state's infrastructure could handle another disaster. It is crucial we learn from our mistakes. Our world must be prepared for more unstable weather.

The good news is that people all over the world are preparing for climate change. A student in India created a

BEST AND WORST PLACES

Although we are all affected by climate change and extreme weather, we are not all affected equally. Scientists predict that Ireland, Sweden, Greenland, and Russian Siberia will be the least damaged by climate change. In the United States, the state best suited to handle climate change is Michigan; Florida is the least suited.

Island countries, coastal areas, and countries close to the equator will be the hardest hit. African countries, despite contributing the least to climate change, will be severely affected. The Philippines, southeast Asian countries, and Middle Eastern countries also have higher risks of damage because of extreme heat. Helping to fight climate change is also helping them.

solar-powered cart so street vendors can work without burning wood or coal. People in Chicago are turning empty lots into farms to feed themselves. Fishermen in Greece are being paid to remove plastic from the ocean. Millions of people want to fight climate change and there are millions of ways they can help.

The End, or the Beginning?

There is no "Planet B." If we are going to have a future, we have to fight for a healthy Earth.

Although climate change has begun, we can protect what we have and avoid making it worse. Climate change crosses borders, so we all have to fight it together. Don't let this be the end of your fight.

Make it the beginning.

CALL TO ACTION!

BE PREPARED

Climate change affects everyone, so we all need to understand it. Include as many people as possible in your club. Help your town plan for droughts and make plans in case of a climate disaster; be prepared. Encourage your city and country to invest in adaptation and resiliency measures, like flood controls and alternative energy sources.

No matter what you do to help fight climate change, be sure that your parents or an adult as well as your school know what you are doing and agree with your plans; never do anything by yourself.

AUTHOR'S NOTE

Earth's climate is changing quickly and some of the numbers and words in this book may not reflect all those changes. But the ideas in this book and the actions you can take will stay the same. Remember that group actions have a big impact. You can try to get your school, your family, the town or city where you live, and your local, state, and federal governments involved in anything you believe in, and in any actions you want to take.

GLOSSARY

....

acid rain: Rainwater that is slightly acidic. It can kill plants and destroy soil.

algae: Tiny living things that use photosynthesis to produce their own food and absorb carbon dioxide. Too many algae in one place can cause eutrophication.

anthropogenic: Caused by humans.

aquifers: Supplies of freshwater that exist underground, trapped between rocks.

atmosphere: The mass of air that surrounds Earth. It includes the air we breathe.

axis: An imaginary line that the earth spins around. It connects the north and south poles.

biodegradable: Able to break down by itself in nature. All living things are all biodegradable.

biodiversity: A measurement of how many different species of plants and animals are in one place. Healthy ecosystems are biodiverse.

biomagnification: When many small animals eat a form of pollution, such as microplastics, and those small animals are in turn eaten by larger animals, which then absorb all the pollution from those small animals.

carbon: An element that is in all living things and also found in coal, oil, natural gas, and diamonds.

carbon footprint: The total sum of carbon dioxide and other greenhouse gases produced by one person, town, country, or business. A bigger footprint has a bigger impact on climate change.

chemicals: Substances that cannot be broken down without changing into something else. When two or more chemicals interact and change into something else, it is called a chemical reaction. The term "chemicals" is sometimes used to refer to substances used in factories that may be dangerous to living things.

climate: The overall trend of a region's temperature, precipitation, wind, and moisture. Climate happens over a long time.

climate change: A global trend affecting both climate and weather.

climate refugees: Also called climate migrants; people forced to leave their homes because of the effects of climate change.

concentrated animal feeding operation (CAFO): A method of growing livestock by keeping animals close together and feeding them grains; also called factory farming.

continents: Giant landmasses. There are seven continents on Earth: Africa, Antarctica, Asia, Australia, Europe, North America, and South America.

crust: The earth's surface or outer layer.

decomposition: When organic matter breaks down into smaller pieces.

deforestation: The removal of forests from land so that it can be used for other things.

ecosystems: Communities of organisms and their environments—like the water, soil, and climate—functioning as ecological units.

ecosystem services: Benefits naturally provided by the plants and animals living in a habitat, such as producing fruit or filtering water.

ecotourism: Touring natural habitats in a way that minimizes ecological impact.

emissions: Substances discharged into the air.

endangered: Close to extinction.

energy: Usable power such as heat or electricity.

energy density: How much energy something has compared to how much it weighs.

environments: The conditions by which you are surrounded; can also refer to all of nature on Earth.

equator: An imaginary circular line around the earth midway between the northern and southern hemispheres; average temperatures near the equator are generally higher than on other parts of the planet.

erosion: The wearing down of the earth's surface; the process by which soil and rock are removed by wind, water, and ice.

eutrophication: When a body of water receives too many dissolved nutrients, causing the growth of algae and resulting in loss of dissolved oxygen.

evaporates: Changes from a liquid to a vapor.

extinction: The process by which a species disappears completely from existence.

fertilizers: Substances used to make soil more fertile; a natural fertilizer is manure. Chemical fertilizers are made in factories.

fossil fuels: Substances made from fossilized plant and animal remains such as petroleum (oil), coal, and natural gas; when burned, they release carbon dioxide, a greenhouse gas, into the air. Fossil fuels are used to power industry and transportation.

fresh water: Water without salt.

glaciers: Large bodies of ice.

Green Revolution: The birth of modernized industrial agriculture, due to pesticides and good management systems.

greenhouse effect: When gases in the atmosphere trap heat, allowing the earth to warm up enough to sustain life. Currently, the greenhouse effect is becoming stronger, increasing the temperature on Earth.

greenhouse gases: Natural and human-made gases in the atmosphere responsible for the greenhouse effect.

groundwater: Water trapped underground between rocks and soil. A body of groundwater is called an aquifer.

habitats: The places where an animal or a plant naturally lives and grows.

indigenous: Someone or something that lives and occurs natively in a region or environment.

infertility: The inability to produce offspring.

life cycle assessment: A calculation of the total environmental cost of a product, from basic ingredients to final disposal.

microplastics: Tiny pieces of plastic that are invisible to the naked eye.

natural gas: A gas that comes from the earth's crust through a natural opening or a well made by people.

neurological damage: Abnormalities to nerves and the brain, affecting bodies.

nonrenewable resources: Natural resources that cannot be duplicated quickly, such as fossil fuels.

nutrients: Substances that give nourishment.

ocean current: A movement of water created by wind, water temperature, the amount of salt in the water, and gravity of the moon.

ozone: A naturally occurring gas that, at ground level, causes smog and is bad for living things. High in the atmosphere, it protects Earth from the sun's harmful rays.

pesticides: Substances used to destroy pests.

photosynthesis: The process by which plants and algae use the sun's heat and light to make their own food.

pollutants: Things that cause pollution.

pollution: Environmental contamination.

precipitation: Hail, mist, rain, sleet, or snow.

prehistoric: Taking place before written history.

protein: A naturally occurring substance in food that the human body needs to function.

reforestation: Renewing forests by planting seeds or young trees.

renewable resources: Useful substances that replace themselves naturally, such as wind or water.

resiliency: The ability to recover from or adjust easily to change.

runoff: Water that drains away.

salt water: Ocean water; water with salt in it.

sediment: Layers of sand, mud, and solid materials such as very small or very large rocks and remains of plants and animals that fall to the bottom of a body of water.

sinks: Oceans, trees, and other natural parts of the environment that take greenhouse gases out of the atmosphere.

smog: A fog made heavier and darker by smoke and chemical fumes.

soil: The upper layer of the earth, where plants grow.

source: Something that produces greenhouse gases, such as cars, factories, or cows.

soybeans: The fruit or seed of the soy plant; a common crop.

sustainability: The practice of harvesting or using a resource so it is not depleted.

sustainable agriculture: Farming practices that reduce the overall environmental impact.

tectonic plates: Pieces of the earth's crust and the part just under it that have been moving very slowly for billions of years.

temperatures: Measurements of heat and cold on a definite scale.

time scale: The rate at which time passes.

unequal heating: The solar heating of the earth's surface, causing air to move.

vegan: A person who does not eat any animal products.

vegetarian: A person who does not eat any meat.

water vapor: The gaseous phase of water.

weather: The state of the atmosphere in a particular place or time regarding temperature, wetness, calmness, or clearness.

RECOMMENDED READING

The Earthworks Group. *The New 50 Simple Things Kids Can Do to Save the Earth*. Kansas City: Andrews McMeel, 2009.

Fritz, Joanne Rossmassler. *Everywhere Blue*. New York: Holiday House, 2021.

Herman, Gail. *What Is Climate Change?* New York: Penguin Workshop, 2018.

Hiaasen, Carl. *Hoot*. New York: Alfred A. Knopf, 2002.

Klein, Naomi, and Rebecca Stefoff. *How to Change Everything: The Young Human's Guide to Protecting the Planet and Each Other*. New York: Atheneum Books for Young Readers, 2021.

Rosenberg, Madelyn. *One Small Hop*. New York: Scholastic, 2021.

Scaletta, Kurtis. *Rooting for Rafael Rosales*. Chicago: Albert Whitman & Company, 2017.

Simon, Seymour. *Climate Action: What Happened and What We Can Do*. New York, Harper. 2021.

Thunberg, Greta. *No One Is Too Small to Make a Difference*. New York: Penguin Books. 2019.

Zissu, Alexandra. *Earth Squad: 50 People Who Are Saving the Planet*. Philadelphia: Running Press, 2021.